'I'm a massive fan of these two blokes. They cut through the jargon to help anyone switch from being a saver to an investor. Saving to invest is how real wealth is built.'

DAVID KOCH, TV PRESENTER

'I wish I'd read this book 15 years ago! A perfect start for any beginner who is thinking about investing. It's a must-read for anyone who's scared of the stock market, like I was.'

USMAN KHAWAJA, AUSTRALIAN TEST CRICKETER

'*Get Started Investing* demystifies investing and makes achieving financial freedom practicable without a huge pay packet. Whether you're 16 or 61, Ren and Bryce will empower you to stop living pay cheque to pay cheque and leave money anxiety behind.'

ALISHA AITKEN-RADBURN, COMMUNICATIONS CONSULTANT
AND FORMER *BACHELOR* STAR

'Bryce and Alec have completed the must-read A to Z guide of how to not only start investing, but how to stay the course to make you money, using expert opinions, personal anecdotes and their own experiences to bring the topic to life.'

DANIELLE ECUYER, FOUNDER OF SHAREPLICITY

'Investing is an important life skill that is not taught in school. With *Get Started Investing*, Alec and Bryce take readers on a journey from actionable ways people can get started to helpful investing lessons from experts.'

TED RICHARDS, FORMER AFL PLAYER WITH ESSENDON BOMBERS AND SYDNEY
SWANS, NOW HEAD OF DISTRIBUTION AT SIX PARK ASSET MANAGEMENT

T0357923

What the readers are saying

'Great book if you're someone looking to start investing for the very first time.' *Goodreads*

'I've bought many books and listened to many podcasts about the share market. This book sums up everything I've read and learnt to date. Ren and Bryce explain things in non-jargon language, that anyone can understand.' *Booktopia*

'A terrific book for those starting out or part way down their journey into investing . . . I have read a number of investing books and this is the easiest to digest with just enough information to get you through without it reading like a textbook.' *Amazon*

'Honestly, one of the easiest to read books I've ever read. If you've ever had an interest in investing but have been too scared to start—Get Started Investing.' *Goodreads*

'This is a great book to help you understand the basics of investing. And it inspires you to get started!' *Booktopia*

'Highly recommend for all ages from 15 to 65!! All explained in simple terminology and "No Jargon"!!' *Amazon*

'If you're interested in investing and don't have any knowledge of the share market this is a good place to start . . . I had no money invested and not a lot to spare. Three months later I have over $5,000 invested and am not scared when things dip.' *Booktopia*

'It is one of best books on investing for beginners and focuses on value investing for the long term.' *Amazon*

Get
Started
Investing

It's easier than you think to invest in shares

**Alec Renehan
& Bryce Leske
Equity**Mates

ALLEN&UNWIN
SYDNEY • MELBOURNE • AUCKLAND • LONDON

First published in 2021

Copyright © Alec Renehan and Bryce Leske 2021

Equity Mates Media operates under Australian Financial Services Licence 540697

Allen & Unwin
83 Alexander Street
Crows Nest NSW 2065
Australia
Phone: (61 2) 8425 0100
Email: info@allenandunwin.com
Web: www.allenandunwin.com

 A catalogue record for this book is available from the National Library of Australia

ISBN 978 1 76087 992 1

Internal design by Simon Paterson and Samantha Collins, Bookhouse
Illustrations by Cohen Gum
Index by Puddingburn
Set in 12/16 pt Adobe Garamond Pro by Bookhouse, Sydney
Printed and bound in Australia by the Opus Group

15 14 13 12 11 10

 The paper in this book is FSC® certified. FSC® promotes environmentally responsible, socially beneficial and economically viable management of the world's forests.

To our parents and partners, for believing in us.
To our friends, for tolerating us.
To the Equity Mates community, for indulging us.

None of this would be possible without you.

Finally, to Warren Buffett.
Hopefully this dedication gets you to reply to our letters.

In the spirit of reconciliation, we would like to begin by acknowledging and paying respect to Australia's Aboriginal and Torres Strait Islander peoples, the traditional custodians of Country throughout Australia, and acknowledging their connections to land, sea and community. We pay respect to their Elders, past, present and emerging, and extend that respect to all Aboriginal and Torres Strait Islander peoples today.

Contents

Part 1 Introduction

Part 2 Why Invest?

Part 3 Build an Investor Mindset

Part 4 Get Your Money Right

Part 5 Understanding the Basics

Part 6 Taking the Plunge

Part 7 Beyond the First Investment

Part 8　Lessons We Wish We Had Known

Part 9　Pulling It All Together

Introduction

The investing world can be big and confusing.
That's why every new investor needs an equity mate.

Welcome

Investing. Getting started is not as hard as you think.

It's a daunting idea, seen as a lot of work to understand the markets and a lot of risk for your hard-earned money. We never learn about it in school and it can be hard to learn yourself, with all the charts, data and jargon. For many people, it feels overwhelming, daunting and ends up in the too-hard basket.

That's unfortunate, because the stock market is an amazing wealth-creating machine. It's our opportunity to invest in some of the smartest people, in some of the best companies and in the cutting edge of innovation.

There's a lot of noise out there. Our perception of investing from movies and TV is fast-paced day trading, shouting across crowded trading floors or spending days sitting in front of multiple computer monitors.

The good news is you can forget all that.

Investing in shares makes you a part-owner of a company. That company is created to earn a profit for its owners (i.e. you!). You don't need to plant yourself in front of a computer for hours a day. You don't need to check your investments daily, weekly or every monthly. Some of the most successful investors have bought great companies and then done nothing for decades. They simply buy a good company and then let that company's management do all the work. That's an opportunity we should all be taking advantage of!

So welcome to *Get Started Investing*, and the beginning of your journey. By the end of this book you will have the information, confidence and, most importantly, the inspiration to get started investing.

How to read this book

Get Started Investing is split into a number of sections—starting with why investing is a critical life skill, then getting into what the stock market is and then how you can access it. Throughout the book there will be lessons from expert investors and from everyday people like you to help you learn from their experience, mistakes and successes.

As you read this book you'll come across a few different boxes, each identified by an icon. This is what they mean.

Pardon the jargon

As you start learning about investing, you'll come across a lot of new terms. Don't be put off. We'll be explaining them all in these 'Pardon the jargon' boxes throughout *Get Started Investing*.

Listener questions

Every investor was a beginner at one stage. Many of us had the same questions that you have today. We've pulled out some of the most common questions on the basics of investing from the Equity Mates community and answered them throughout *Get Started Investing*.

From the Equity Mates community

Learning from the experiences of others is a great way to get started. Throughout *Get Started Investing* we're featuring some of the learnings, experiences and mistakes from the Equity Mates community so you can see how others started their investing journeys.

From the experts

We've spoken to over 150 expert investors since we started Equity Mates. It has been one of the most valuable ways we've learned about the stock market. Throughout *Get Started Investing* we've featured some of the most important insights we've gained from these experts so you can learn from them as well.

Who are we?

We are Bryce and Alec, the co-founders of Equity Mates, the #1 finance and investing brand for young Australians. What started as a podcast tracking our journey of learning to invest has grown into a community of everyday investors looking to learn more about the market and get smarter with their money.

We met at university and developed an interest in investing. But it was challenging to know where to start. There wasn't a lot of easy-to-understand content out there for people like us. As we spoke to family and friends we realised a lot of people faced the same challenges. We all knew investing was something we *should* do, but it was difficult to work out *how* to do it. Financial markets were seen as complex and inaccessible, and financial media catered to the industry but not everyday Australians.

We set out to record our journey of learning to invest in the hope others would join. Equity Mates Investing Podcast started in 2017 and, in the years since, has grown a community of young investors in Australia and around the world. In 2019, we launched a second podcast—*Get Started Investing*—as a complement to Equity Mates Investing Podcast.

Over the journey we've interviewed some of the biggest names in finance and beyond, everyone from former prime minister Malcolm Turnbull to AFL footballer Chris Judd, from the face of Australian financial reporting Alan Kohler to cricketer Usman Khawaja. With more than 6 million downloads and a community of more than a hundred thousand everyday investors, we have a mission to make markets accessible and give you the information and confidence to get started.

FROM THE EQUITY MATES
community

'My favourite podcast yet. Has helped me immensely with investing. Especially love the interview style and thought-provoking questioning. Amazing!! Keep up the great work.'
CHARLOTTE C T VIA APPLE PODCASTS

'If it weren't for this podcast I wouldn't have started investing! Thanks for all the knowledge you have provided!'
JOELLECLOW VIA APPLE PODCASTS

'You guys are the best—no other way to put it. Love your intelligent discussion and education while incorporating banter and keeping it down to earth and simple. Keep it up guys, thanks so much.'
RUDEVICS VIA APPLE PODCASTS

'These guys were the catalyst that kickstarted my investing journey. Love the diverse range of perspectives that are interviewed. Both hosts have a wealth of knowledge and have a great ability to articulate how multifaceted the market is.'
SHILLY 123 VIA APPLE PODCASTS

Our personal investing journeys

ALEC

Investing isn't something that came naturally to me.

My family, like so many Australian families, saw property as the way you built wealth. You saved for a deposit, bought a house and then paid off your mortgage. The Australian dream.

When I started investing, I had no idea what I was doing. My first investment—I lost all my money. Well, that's a slight exaggeration. I managed to turn $1,000 into $12. You can't have a worse start to investing than me!

For some reason (blind optimism probably) I stuck with it. I was working a part-time job while studying and just kept saving a bit every pay until I was ready to invest again. Then I did it again, and again, and again.

Over the journey I kept making mistakes, but kept at it. Kept learning and kept saving. There is no trick to investing, no perfect set of steps to take or books to read to become a stock market genius.

At the same time, there is nothing stopping anyone from getting started. While it seems like there are so many reasons everyday people can't invest themselves, it is within anyone's grasp to get started. My journey is an example of that.

 BRYCE

From a very young age my parents tried to teach me the value of money.

I was lucky enough to receive a small amount of pocket money—$1.50 every fortnight, early on in my schooling life.

This was to be split into three: 50 cents into a 'spending' jar (used to buy fish food for my two goldfish, or the occasional Fizzer from the school canteen); 50 cents into a 'savings' jar (from memory I bought a bodyboard after yeeeeears of saving); and finally, 50 cents into an 'investing' jar.

It was the investing jar that was the catalyst for the journey I have been on since. Once I'd saved the minimum $500 required to invest, which was by the start of high school, we invested it into a listed investment company (LIC).

Of course, I had no idea what that meant, or where my money had actually gone. Dad showed me how to track the share price of the company in the paper (come on, there were no apps!), and from that moment I was hooked.

It sparked my interest in shares and investing, and, more broadly, in business and finance.

I've made my fair share of mistakes. I've chased fortune and glory, investing in companies I'd never heard of, only to lose almost everything. I've actually done that a few times, whoops . . . but now I've learnt my lesson.

I believe investing is a critical life skill. It's a skill that doesn't require a degree. If by the end of *Get Started Investing* we've inspired just one person to start their journey, then that's all we can ask for.

Why did we write
Get Started Investing?

For you!

We've been through the challenges every beginner faces. We've asked the same questions and gone through the process of trying to make sense of all the information out there. We wanted to get started, but the question was always: how?

We hope *Get Started Investing* can be the answer for people currently asking this question. It is a summary of everything we've learnt through our journey of learning to invest. We've made plenty of mistakes, spoken to some of the best investors in Australia and around the world, and learnt from our community of everyday investors. *Get Started Investing* takes a step-by-step approach to the process of getting started and includes plenty of lessons we wish we had known when we were starting out.

Investing is a lifelong journey and we hope that *Get Started Investing* will give you the information, confidence and inspiration to start that journey today.

PART 2

Why Invest?

Investing is an incredibly important life skill for every Australian.
Here is why we believe you should start your investing journey.

Why we invest

Asking why someone invests probably seems like a silly question.

To make more money of course.

I guess we should ask: why do you want to make more money?

There are plenty of reasons to start investing. Some people want to set themselves up for a comfortable retirement. Others want to retire as soon as possible. Some people want to have the money to buy a house. Others want to be able to buy their kids a house.

To kick off this section, we want to share why we invest.

Why I invest

ALEC

The #1 reason I invest is for financial freedom.

Not the 'retired and sitting on a beach' kind of freedom or the 'flying my private jet to my private island' kind of freedom either (although, it would be nice . . .). No, I invest for the freedom to have choices about where and how I work in the future.

I love the idea of being able to do a job I am passionate about even if it pays a little less. Or being able to take a career break to spend more time with my family. I love the idea of having choices and flexibility.

To do that, I need to set myself up financially, so I invest to give my future self options.

What I've found is that through learning about investing, I've learnt more about the world. I've learnt about industries I wouldn't otherwise know the first thing about. I've learnt about people doing really interesting things and trying to solve really hard problems.

Investing has made me a more curious person, which has helped me in my day job. It has allowed me to understand what is out there and helped me think about what I want to do with the rest of my life.

BRYCE

The obvious answer: to make money! But if I peel that back a layer, the real answer is very similar to Alec's.

The idea of investing is to put your hard-earned money to work, to let it grow, to produce an income stream, so that eventually you don't need to rely on someone else to pay you.

I invest so that in the future I'm able to take advantage of new opportunities. I invest so in the future I'm not tied to a salary. I invest to give myself the best chance of living on my terms.

The crazy thing? It's not wildly unachievable. The stock market provides amazing opportunities to build wealth, particularly over the long term.

I also invest because it's insanely fun! It makes me view and question the world around us in ways I would never have imagined. I'm constantly learning, and developing as a better investor. It's a lifelong journey, and I'll likely never perfect the art. Many, many professionals don't. But the process, and the goal at the end, is so worthwhile.

FROM THE EQUITY MATES
community

We asked our community why they invest. Among the responses, there were some clear themes that came back. The desire to be financially free; wanting to provide for their family; and a more financially secure retirement.

'To be able to support myself financially in the future and save money for my future kids!'
ALESIA

'To create a portfolio to complement my super funds at retirement.'
DANIEL

'My investing goal is to retire younger than the average age. I think it's important to set an amount of money to invest periodically from your pay cheque and make it a habit.'
MAURICIO

'Build wealth to hopefully live a comfortable life. Not super rich, just a yearly overseas holiday and not feeling pressure with money.'
MEL

'I want to be in a position before retirement where I don't have to work for money, and can make decisions based on what I feel is good for me and my family.'
MICHAEL

'I'm keen to grow wealth so I can rely less on salaries as I get older, and give my kids something to keep investing or use to buy their first homes.'
SIMON

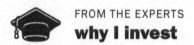

FROM THE EXPERTS
why I invest

Jessica Amir is a market analyst at Bell Direct.

'Why do I invest? Well, primarily, it's to grow my little pennies . . .'

Jessica then went on to remind us about what we're doing when we're investing. We're creating other opportunities to make money outside our own work and our own career.

'It's all about backing a story for me . . . if you can make money from someone else making money, it's a win–win. So I think that's what it's all about, just benefiting from someone else's success, backing someone else in.'

Paul Wilson is an Australian technology investor, and the co-founder and managing partner at Bailador Technology Investments. Paul has had a long history investing in and growing Australian technology businesses.

'I began to invest, specifically targeting venture capital growth companies, private companies. Part of the reason was I grew up in Queensland. I was seeing businesses that were getting to a certain stage and just getting taken over. And so I thought, oh, what can we do to help these businesses [to] just keep growing and employing people in the local community and then become successful on the global stage? And so that germ of an idea really took hold in my early twenties and it's kind of been my North Star ever since . . .

[I'm] pleased to say that we now have a track record of helping lots of Australian businesses go and conquer the world, become world leaders in their segment, employ thousands of people and contribute to a vibrant tech and tech business sector here in Australia. So that's really the thing that gets me out of bed and excites me about what we do.'

The biggest risk is not investing

The #1 reason that people don't start investing is that they worry the stock market is 'too risky'. But, when you start to understand the awesome wealth-creating power of the stock market, the biggest risk may be missing out.

The stock market is often seen as a big risk. Many people have heard stories of the major market crashes throughout history—the 1929 Great Depression, the 2000 Tech Wreck, the 2008 Global Financial Crisis (GFC). We've also heard the stories of individual companies collapsing and investors losing all their money—Enron and Lehman Brothers in America, Ansett Australia and Dick Smith Electronics in Australia. In 2020, many notable companies collapsed during the Covid-19 pandemic, including Australian airline Virgin Australia and global car rental giant Hertz.

These stories make us concerned that we'll lose our hard-earned money. We don't want to be working long hours at our 9–5 job, only to see savings lost by a risky stock market investment.

Instead, we choose to save our money in the bank. Saving and saving. Focusing on cutting our expenses, and saving our way to a comfortable retirement.

Unfortunately, saving your money in the bank can be a bigger risk. Your money can actually lose value over time. This introduces the first piece of jargon that you need to understand: **inflation**.

PARDON THE JARGON
inflation

Inflation measures the amount prices for goods and services increase. If it used to cost $2 to buy 1 litre of milk and a loaf of bread from the shops, and it now costs $3, that rise in prices is referred to as inflation. Over time prices generally rise and this means each of our dollars purchases less.

In Australia, between 1951 and 2020, prices have risen an average of 4.9% every year. This means every year your $1 buys 4.9% less in goods and services. Or in practical terms, if you're stashing all your cash under your mattress and not earning any interest, $100 could buy you 100 litres of milk when it was $1 a litre. As prices increase and milk goes to $1.10 a litre, that $100 buys only 90 litres of milk. The same amount of money buys less.

Think about the stories your grandparents would tell you about buying a meat pie for 10 cents. Now you'll be lucky to get one for $4. That's inflation.

At the very least, you want your savings to keep up with inflation. If prices inflate at 1% in a year, you need to earn at least 1% interest just to buy the same amount of stuff. Unfortunately, most bank savings accounts these days pay less than the historical average for inflation.

Forget what you've heard—cash is not king.

You may be thinking, 'So what? As long as I've got a job and am earning a salary, I'll be okay.' Unfortunately, this becomes a problem in retirement. Most Australians—60%—run out of money before they die, and the average Australian outlives their retirement savings by five years. Making your money work for you while you're young is the best way to ensure you'll have the retirement you want.

While saving your money in a bank or under your mattress may feel like the least risk, it may be the riskiest option for your future self.

FROM THE EXPERTS
savings versus investment

Robert G. Allen is an investment adviser and personal finance author. He asks a question that always reminds us of the importance of investing to set ourselves up for retirement.

'How many millionaires do you know who have become wealthy by investing in savings accounts?
I rest my case.'

FROM THE EQUITY MATES
community

'I had started to save some money and realised that it was doing nothing for me in the bank . . . I realised it was actually losing value to inflation.'
JAMES

'I always thought investing in stocks was risky. Now I know not investing is far more dangerous when it comes to achieving long-term goals and lifelong wealth.'
JONO

The cost of missed opportunity

Every dollar you earn from your job offers a choice. You can spend it, you can save it or you can invest it. The difference between the choice you made and the choice you didn't is called 'opportunity cost'.

If you are choosing to save your money rather than invest it, it may feel safe today but there is a big opportunity cost in your future.

Don't save to save. Save to invest, and make your money work for you. Throughout *Get Started Investing* we'll show you how.

Compounding

Since the creation of the first company, investing in companies has been a powerful creator of wealth for millions of people. A lot of this is due to the awesome power of compounding.

You've decided that keeping your money in the bank isn't the right call. You need a way for your money to work for you, to earn interest and stay ahead of inflation. The reason investing is the right call is the awesome power of compounding.

 FROM THE EXPERTS
the importance of compounding

Albert Einstein was not an investor, but rather a theoretical physicist who developed the theory of relativity. A famous quote that recognises the power of compounding is often attributed to him.

> 'Compound interest is the eighth wonder of the world. He who understands it, earns it; he who doesn't, pays it.'

Einstein isn't the only famous historical figure who understood the power of compound interest. **Benjamin Franklin**, one of the Founding Fathers of the United States, similarly understood its importance.

> 'Money makes money. And the money that money makes, makes money.'

FROM THE EQUITY MATES
community

We asked our community some of the key lessons they've learned since they started investing. For Simone, the power of compounding was a big one.

'Compounding to create a passive income is truly powerful. [I] did not quite realise this at the start.'

Compound interest is a term we all learn at school, and a lot of us promptly forget. It is important to remind ourselves what it means.

Interest is the money we earn on our money (e.g. your bank pays you interest on your savings account). There are two types of interest: **simple interest** and **compound interest**.

PARDON THE JARGON
simple interest and compound interest

Simple interest is where you earn money on the money you put in at the start. For example, if you invest $100 and have a 10% interest rate, every year you get paid $10 (10% of $100).

Compound interest is where you earn money on the money you put in at the start and all interest you are paid. For example, if you invest $100 and have a 10% *compound* interest rate, the first year you get paid $10 (same as simple interest). But you then have $110, so in the second year you earn interest on the $110, so get paid $11 (10% of $110). In year 3, you get paid $12.10 (10% of $121) and it would keep growing from there.

With compound interest you make money on the money you earn. It is a virtuous cycle where a small investment can grow into a very large amount over a long period of time.

Take the example of someone who invests $100 and earns 10% interest. With simple interest you get paid $10 every year. With compound interest the amount you get paid increases every year. Over time a big difference starts to emerge:

	Simple interest	Compound interest
Year 1	$10	$10.00
Year 2	$10	$11.00
Year 3	$10	$12.10
Year 4	$10	$13.31
Year 5	$10	$14.64
Year 6	$10	$16.11
Year 7	$10	$17.72
Year 8	$10	$19.49
Year 9	$10	$21.44
Year 10	$10	$23.58
Year 11	$10	$25.94
Year 12	$10	$28.53
Year 13	$10	$31.38
Year 14	$10	$34.52
Year 15	$10	$37.97
Year 16	$10	$41.77
Year 17	$10	$45.95
Year 18	$10	$50.54
Year 19	$10	$55.60
Year 20	$10	$61.16
Total earned	$200	$572.75

The benefits of time

Compound interest gets particularly interesting if you can earn a consistent rate of interest over a long period of time.

As the returns grow year after year, the numbers start getting exciting.

Take our $100 invested at 10% as an example:

- If you invest $100 at 10% for five years, you will multiply your money by 1.6 times (you will have $161).
- If you invest that money at that 10% for ten times as long (50 years rather than five), you will not multiply your wealth by sixteen times . . . you will multiply it by more than 117 times (you will have more than $10,000!).

This is because the growth of this money is exponential. By year 50, you are not just earning money on your original investment, you are also earning money on the previous 49 years' returns. Your money is making money that is making money.

The stock market is the ultimate compounding machine

The way you make money in the stock market is through this compound interest principle. Over time, companies invent new products and services, expand to new markets and grow in value. They get more valuable and then grow again and then some more.

How companies compound

HOW COMPANIES GROW

And so on...

The new staff create more products and make more money

The company sells the product and uses the profits to hire new staff

A product is created by a company

Over the past 40 years, the Australian market has averaged 11% growth per year and the US market has averaged 12% growth per year. You can see in the table below how this has compounded wealth for investors.

How investors' money has grown over the last 40 years

If you'd invested $1,000 in Australia (Index: All Ordinaries Total Return)		If you'd invested $1,000 in the USA (Index: S&P 500 Total Return)	
Start of 1980	$1,000	Start of 1980	$1,000
1989	$5,088	1989	$5,037
1999	$14,427	1999	$26,836
2009	$33,688	2009	$24,389
2019	$71,800	2019	$86,984

The first thing we notice when we look at the numbers in the table is that, between 1999 and 2009 in the United States, our investor lost money.

- In 1999, at the height of the frenzy over the first generation of internet companies, our investor had $27k.
- By 2009, the middle of the US housing crisis, our investor had $24k.

Over ten years, they had lost $3,000. Not ideal. We'll explain everything you need to know about stock market crashes later in this section. For now, just look at this fall in the context of how the starting $1,000 had grown. This market fall was a minor hiccup in some incredible growth. Our investor's money was able to compound year after year into a serious amount of money.

This awesome power of compounding is why the stock market has been such an effective creator of wealth for so many investors. It's not about day trading or finding the perfect stock; it's just been about earning a consistent return over a long period of time.

Buy and hold. Set and forget. Thanks to the effect of compounding returns, this is all you have to do.

WARREN BUFFETT
meet history's greatest investor

Warren Buffett is arguably the greatest investor in history. At 90 years old, after a lifetime of investing, he was worth $86 billion!

Buffett's life story is the story of compounding returns.

As he earned a consistent rate of return on his money, it grew and grew.

At 50, he was worth only $100 million ('only' being a relative term here). Forty years later—when he reached 90—his wealth had increased a staggering 800 times to $86 billion.

Buffett's net worth

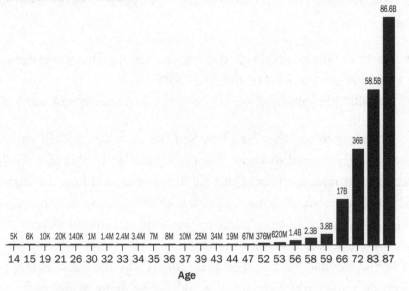

Age

Buffett's investing philosophy

Buffett got incredibly rich with an incredibly simple philosophy: find really good businesses and hold them for a really long period of time. Let compounding do its thing.

Here are some of our favourite quotes from history's greatest investor:

'When we own portions of outstanding businesses with outstanding managements, our favourite holding period is forever.'

'All there is to investing is picking good stocks at good times and staying with them as long as they remain good companies.'

'I never attempt to make money on the stock market. I buy on the assumption that they could close the market the next day and not reopen it for five years.'

Some of the shares Buffett bought

- Coca-Cola—held since 1988
- American Express—held since 1963
- Gillette—held since 1989 (until company sold to Procter & Gamble in 2005)
- Wells Fargo—held since 1989
- *The Washington Post*—held since 1973 (until company sold to Jeff Bezos in 2013)

Stop relying on your pay

*For most people, their main source of income is their salary.
Investing gives you another source of income and another way
to build wealth.*

The traditional way most people build wealth is to get a job, start saving, try to negotiate a pay rise or promotion every now and then, eventually buy a house and, hopefully, retire with enough money saved and in superannuation to enjoy retirement.

There's nothing wrong with this plan; we just think there is a better one.

Historically, the stock market has grown a lot quicker than workers' pay. While the Australian stock market has averaged a 13% increase year after year since 1900, no one is getting a 13% pay rise every year at work. The numbers out of the United States tell the extreme version of this story.

FROM THE EXPERTS
the wealth created by the stock market

Patrick O'Shaughnessy is the author of one of our favourite investing books, *Millennial Money* (a great book, with a terrible title!). In this book he explained the difference in rises in worker pay and the stock market.

For workers

'Between 1974 and 2011, real income [income after inflation] rose by a tiny 3.2% for the vast majority of Americans, while real income grew by 154% for the top-earning 1%.'

Compared to the stock market

'Luckily, there is a simple solution. An investment in the stock market in 1974—the beginning of this period of income stagnation—would have made the growth of income for even the top earners look pedestrian. Between 1974 and 2011, when the average worker barely earned a raise, the stock market grew by a real 759% [after inflation].'

We aren't saying don't ask for that pay rise at work. We're just saying don't go all-in on that strategy!

More importantly, investing your money early in your life gives you more flexibility later on. Growing your wealth through investing means you don't need to rely on your salary to cover your bills and expenses. You will be able to sell some of your investments to cover these costs.

The flexibility investing gives you means you can leave a job you hate without worrying about how you'll pay the bills. It means you can take a lower paying job doing something that interests you. It allows you to take a break from work, or take longer parental leave. The freedom of not having to rely on your salary in the future is why we invest today.

The Equity Mates community is full of people who are learning to invest now, so they give themselves flexibility later on in life.

 FROM THE EQUITY MATES
community

We asked the community about their investing goals: basically, why they invest.

A lot of the responses we received were focused on financial freedom and being able to break out of the 9–5 rat race. Basically, to not be solely reliant on their salary.

'I decided to start investing so I'm not reliant on a pay cheque in 20–30 years' time and have some sort of financial freedom when making decisions in life.'

MICHAEL

'Basically, I want to be in a position where I can retire as young as possible and have more control and flexibility around my future.'
OWEN

'My goal is to build wealth over a long period in the hope of an early retirement. I am also interested in using investing as a hobby and an educational tool.'
PATRICK

'Financial freedom, hopefully an early retirement too.'
SIMONE

FIRE—The ultimate escape from your 9–5

Financial Independence, Retire Early. It's a great aim and a goal for a lot of young people.

Maybe the most extreme reason people invest is to achieve financial independence as soon as possible. This FIRE movement is growing in popularity around the world and focuses on aggressively saving as much as possible by finding ways to increase income and decrease expenses.

This saved money is then invested in assets that pay a **passive income** and allow you to retire early.

 PARDON THE JARGON
passive income

Passive income is income that you don't have to work for. You get paid for doing nothing.

Some classic examples of passive income include:

- rental income from property
- dividends from stocks
- interest from a savings account.

Followers of the FIRE lifestyle focus on minimising their costs in their twenties and thirties so they can enjoy retirement well before the usual retirement age.

Importantly, the goal isn't about stopping work, it's just about not needing to work. You can focus on finding a job you like even if it pays less or finding a cause you're passionate about. You just don't need to take a job because of the pay.

Some of the experts we've interviewed on the podcast love the FIRE movement. But even if you don't want to go to the extreme lengths of the FIRE movement, there's still plenty we can learn from the movement about maximising the amount we save and invest. Throughout *Get Started Investing* we weave in some of the tips and tricks we've picked up from FIRE proponents.

FROM THE EXPERTS
setting FIRE to your investing journey

Pete Matthew is a UK-based chartered financial planner and the managing director of Jacksons Wealth Management. We interviewed him and asked his thoughts on the FIRE movement.

'It's gathering pace, but I think it's potentially one of the most important movements in recent times. I think it'll be hugely important in the next ten years or more. Could have a massive impact on the financial health of an entire generation if it continues to gather pace. It's underrated at the moment, but I'm watching it with huge interest and excitement.'

Andy Hart is the founder of Maven Adviser, a UK-based financial adviser. He shared some of his thoughts on the FIRE movement when we interviewed him.

'The FIRE movement is brilliant. It's quite unique. We have a movement that is peddling wisdom. It's very rare that a movement, and something new, pedals wisdom, they're usually peddling information, they're usually trying to sell things and they're trying to overcomplicate things. This is the opposite. They're trying to demystify finance. They're trying to demystify financial life success.'

FROM THE EXPERTS
achieving financial independence and retiring in your thirties

Chris Reining was living your standard life. Went to university, got a degree and found a job. Then one day, as a 22-year-old sitting in his cubicle at work, he thought 'So I have to do this for 40 more years?' That thought led him to aggressively save and invest and by 37 he had enough money to retire.

We interviewed Chris on the Equity Mates podcast in 2019 and below are some snippets from his interview.

Why Chris decided to follow the FIRE movement

'It wasn't until I was in my late twenties where I sort of looked at my life and figured out that, you know, I can't sit here and do this same job for the next 40 years. And I also don't want to go back to school to do something else or to find an entirely different job in a different field that I might enjoy more. I'd rather just save and invest and put up with the short-term pain. To hopefully someday reach a point where I have enough invested money where I can live off my investments.'

Major lessons

1 MAXIMISE YOUR INCOME FROM YOUR JOB

'I did just have the single income stream. And, you know, I guess I was kind of lucky in the fact that I was working in corporate America. There you have a little bit more flexibility because you can look for raises, you can switch jobs to make more money . . . So for me I guess I realised that my career really was my biggest asset. And the asset that was the best bet for the income stream, versus someone else, who might have to combine a full-time job with a side hustle or two.'

2 TRACK YOUR SPENDING

'I had absolutely no idea where my money was going. And so I took the step of creating a simple spreadsheet to start tracking where my money was going—the money coming in from my pay cheques and the money leaving via paying the bills, paying the rent and all the things that you're spending money on. After doing that for weeks and then months and then what ultimately ended up being years, you start building a picture of where your money is going. And I think just knowing that or actually seeing it on paper was really eye opening because a lot of us just float through life. Money comes in and money leaves and you have really no idea what you're doing with your money. And so I think taking that initial step of writing down how much money was coming in and how much was leaving, I could then target areas where I could potentially save more money.'

3 START WITH SMALL WINS

'When I started out tracking my savings, I think I was saving around 10% of my pay. Probably five years later, I got that up to close to 50%. And then that was just like maxed out. I couldn't really do anything after that. A lot of people probably hear that going from 10% savings rate to 50%—I mean, that's a big, big jump—but it also took me five-plus years to do that . . . It took a lot of discipline and it took a lot of work . . . I think that, one of the first things I did was just start by cutting out something small. So it's kind of like this idea of changing, you're changing a habit. A good way to change your habit is to start with something small rather than trying to start with three huge things. For me, it was something as simple as like, okay, instead of eating lunch out five days a week well I'm just going to eat lunch out four days a week and then three days a week and then two days a week and then one day a week . . . For me, it was almost methodically going through all my different expenses or the ways that I was spending money and figuring out which ones were not getting me towards my goal and I really didn't care about. But then also making sure that I was spending in areas that I got a lot of happiness or pleasure from, like travel. And so I think I was just finding a really good balance between spending and saving in order to sort of increase that savings rate.'

4 AVOID LIFESTYLE CREEP

'. . . it's very common when you're making more and more money to spend more and more money. And so if someone was making $50,000, it's really easy for them to spend $50,000. But that same person, when they're making $100,000, it's somehow very easy for them to spend $100,000. And that just keeps going on and on and on. And that's called lifestyle inflation.'

Forget property

The dream for a lot of young people is to own property. For our parents' and grandparents' generation this was their major investment. However, there are a few reasons why young people should think beyond property.

Owning your own home is the dream for a lot of people. The security of not having to rent is worth chasing. But, as an investment, there are several reasons why property may not be the right decision for a lot of young people today.

Upfront cost

This one almost goes without saying, but buying property is expensive. The process of saving for a deposit can take years, and while you're saving money in the bank, it's not working for you.

Inaccessibility

Buying a house where you want to live can be incredibly expensive. For most young people, it is too expensive, so you settle for where you can afford and subject yourself to a longer commute.

Competition

Negative gearing in Australia allows property investors to claim a tax deduction on the difference between their mortgage payments and rental income. This means you're competing with investors who can afford to pay more because they're willing to make a loss on their rental income.

Ongoing costs

The cost of investing in property doesn't stop when you buy that house. From mortgage repayments to maintenance costs, insurance to council rates, one investment creates a lifetime of costs.

Investing in the stock market doesn't carry any of these headaches. As you'll learn throughout this book, investing in companies is far more accessible than investing in property. You can start with as little as a few cents, have no ongoing maintenance costs or mortgage repayments, and can choose what you buy from behind your computer or phone. No moving vans required.

FROM THE EXPERTS
property versus the stock market

Brandon van der Kolk is the founder of New Money, a financial media company helping Australians take control of their money and achieve financial freedom.

'Australian property is overrated. I don't know too much about property investing, to be perfectly honest. I really like stock market investing. The way I see it is, if you compare the two—Australian property or property in general and [the] stock market—you can get pretty much the same return, if not maybe a bit better. Arguable. Obviously, different stats say different things. But the way I see it, especially if you just want to be someone who invests for the long term and just doesn't have to worry about it too much, then stocks are the way to go. I reckon it's just so simple. And just the amount of stuff that I hear going wrong with property and like, you got to clean the toilets, got to fix the drains. Gotta do this maintenance.'

Andrew Page is the founder and managing director of Strawman.com. He has more than 20 years' experience in financial markets, with experience as an equities analyst and market commentator.

'You know, for so long now I've been pretty negative on Australian property. I always put people offside by saying that. But I would start by saying that property is a fantastic asset. But any asset, you can still do bad in a quality asset if you overpay. And I think the valuation metrics on average—and again, like the share market there are individual exceptions to the wider rule, but I'd say on average—Australian property is well overvalued, it has been for a while and has a lot of systemic risks for the country. So I'd say overrated. The other thing I just add to that as well, you've got horrible liquidity, huge transaction costs and almost no capacity to diversify, unless again, you're extremely wealthy . . .

[W]e've had this scenario now really for the better part of fifteen, almost twenty years we've had this run in the property market that is literally unprecedented in Australia and in global markets over such a timeframe. So there's this idea that it never goes down. It's a sure-fire proposition. And you hear some wonderful success stories. But in that period . . . we've had some other structural factors. The rise of two-income family being a very underrated, under-appreciated one, but also massively increased lending conditions, lower interest rates. All sort of rationally explain what's happened but I think the problem here is that people just push and extrapolate that narrative forward to infinity. And so there's a lot of nuance to unpack with all of that. But I think for those reasons, I think Australians have a perverse view of what is, quote unquote, normal.'

Malcolm Turnbull served as the 29th prime minister of Australia from 2015 to 2018. Prior to his life in politics, he founded the investment bank Whitlam Turnbull & Co., and was the managing director of Goldman Sachs Australia.

'Australian property has been a pretty good one way bet for a very long time but the old story of "don't have all your eggs in one basket" is important to rely on. Diversification is important. Everyone aims to own their own house and obviously get it debt-free as soon as they can because interest on a residential mortgage for your own residence is non-deductible. As your investments grow, if you pour it all into more and more residential property, as some people do, then I think you're concentrating too much in one asset class.'

Perhaps the biggest reason we prefer stocks over property is how you make money on the investment. With property you are buying a piece of land with the expectation that it will get more valuable over time. Nothing about the land itself changes as you own it. You just expect to be able to sell it for more at a later date. Sure you can renovate a house, or subdivide the land, but at the end of the day—if you buy 1 hectare of land you are selling 1 hectare of land and hoping to get a higher price for it. You're speculating about what someone else will be willing to pay in the future.

The stock market is a completely different proposition.

Why stocks?

Unlike property, investing in stocks offers the ability to buy something and watch it turn into something completely different.

With a lot of investments, you are buying something with the expectation that someone will pay more for it later.

- Buy a Picasso? You'd better hope there's an art collector with the money to buy it for more than you paid for it.
- Buy a bar of gold? You're selling a bar of gold at the end of the day, just expecting someone to pay more for it.
- Buy some Bitcoin? The amount of cryptocurrency you bought is the amount you're selling; you're just hoping someone is willing to pay more.
- Even property—the block of land you buy is the block of land you sell. If property values fall, you'll struggle to find someone to pay more for what you own.

That is what makes the stock market unique—why it is, in our opinion, the best option for investing.

You are buying a share in a company that is constantly changing, evolving, growing. What you buy can be completely different from what you sell. The company is managed by a group of people who are applying their ingenuity to develop new products and services, to expand to new countries and to become more productive.

The way to make money in the stock market isn't just by finding someone willing to pay more for the same thing. It is to let the companies themselves actually become more valuable. To wait, as the people running the company find ways to make more profit. To create new products, to expand to new markets and to come up with entirely new businesses. What you eventually sell could be completely different to what you originally bought.

For an example of this, take online retail giant Amazon. If you have owned a share in Amazon since 1997, what you own has completely changed. In 24 years, the business transformed from a bookseller to a cloud computing business and a seller of everything (with a streaming service for good measure).

Chart of Amazon share price since initial public offering

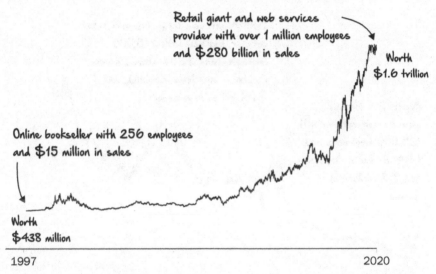

Retail giant and web services provider with over 1 million employees and $280 billion in sales

Worth $1.6 trillion

Online bookseller with 256 employees and $15 million in sales

Worth $438 million

1997   2020

You're not trying to sell a share in an online bookseller for more than you paid for it. You can sell a share in a much bigger, much better and much more valuable company.

Amazon may be the most extreme example of this, but it is the same with every company you can invest in. They all have a strategy to get more productive, to sell more and to make more profit. They are unique in that they are actively working to make your investment more valuable.

Take Woolworths, the Australian supermarket most of us have bought something from at some point. Twenty years ago, it was Australia's largest supermarket. Even starting out as such a big company it has grown and changed over the past two decades. In that time it has tripled the number of stores and expanded into new countries. These businesses are constantly growing and finding ways to make more money for you, as a shareholder.

Essentially, if you invest in a group of companies you are making a bet on the continued innovation and productivity of humanity. That is something that no other investment option offers.

Chart of Woolworths share price over the last twenty years

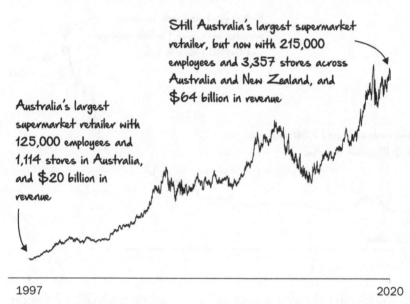

Still Australia's largest supermarket retailer, but now with 215,000 employees and 3,357 stores across Australia and New Zealand, and $64 billion in revenue

Australia's largest supermarket retailer with 125,000 employees and 1,114 stores in Australia, and $20 billion in revenue

1997

2020

Don't work for the company— own the company

Investing in the stock market offers the opportunity to own companies that hire the smartest people, spend billions on research and development and manage global operations all with the aim of returning more money to their shareholders. Don't miss out on that.

Think of some of the biggest innovations of your lifetime. Or some of the biggest innovations in history. Electricity, the telephone, the car, personal computers, online retail.

We hear about the incredible people who invent them: Steve Jobs, Bill Gates and Henry Ford. They become billionaires through their brilliance. We, as everyday investors, have the opportunity to also benefit from their work.

Their innovations have been commercialised and brought to market through publicly traded companies that everyday investors have had the opportunity to invest in.

As investors, we could have benefited from these innovators' work through investing in shares in their companies.

Think about a company you or someone in your family works for. What its purpose is. Why it employs you. At the end of the day, it is to increase profit—make more sales, find more work, cut costs—it is all to finish the day a little more profitable than it started.

The innovators and their companies

Telephone	Electricity	Mass-produced car	Home appliances
Alexander Graham Bell	Thomas Edison	Henry Ford	George Westinghouse
AT&T	General Electric	Ford	Westinghouse Electric

Computer software	Smart phones	Electric cars	Online retail
Bill Gates	Steve Jobs	Elon Musk	Jeff Bezos
Microsoft	Apple	Tesla	Amazon

It is the same for the companies you can invest in through the stock market. These companies are built to earn more profit for their shareholders (owners). The CEOs and executives of these businesses only earn their bonuses if they increase profit, so they go out and hire the smartest people, develop new products and technologies, find new business opportunities and expand into new markets—all to make more profit.

As a shareholder, you are then entitled to a share of this profit.

When you think of it like that, why would you just work for the company when you can own the company?

Investing in tomorrow's big innovations

The really exciting thing about the stock market is that there are always new innovators with new ideas that we can invest in. Think of some of the biggest changes taking place in the world today; there are companies leading the way with new technologies and ideas, trying to solve some of these big problems.

The great news is that we can invest in many of these companies. As everyday people we can benefit from all of their pioneering work by simply buying shares in their companies.

Innovation and a few of the companies working on it

These companies are just to give you a taste of what's out there. We aren't recommending these stocks and the lists are by no means exhaustive.

Space travel and tourism	Virgin Galactic—Space tourism
	Maxar Technologies—Satellites
	Aerojet Rocketdyne—Rocket propulsion
	IHI Corporation—Space launch vehicles
Renewable energy, decarbonising the electricity grid	Iberdrola—Spanish renewable operator
	Vestas Wind Systems—Wind turbines
	First Solar—Solar panels
	Brookfield Renewable—Hydro operator
Finding meat alternatives	Beyond Meat—Plant-based meat
	Impossible Foods—Plant-based meat
	Ingredion—Vegan ingredient supplier
	Tyson—Investor in lab-grown meat start-ups
Artificial intelligence (AI)	NVIDIA—Chip maker
	Alphabet—Large investments in AI
	Alteryx—AI for data science and analytics
	IBM—AI for business
Personalised medicine	CRISPR Therapeutics—Gene editing using CRISPR
	Exact Sciences—Cancer diagnostics
	Illumina—Gene sequencing
	Vertex Pharmaceuticals—Gene therapies
Autonomous vehicles	Tesla—Leader in self-driving technology
	Alphabet—Own Waymo, another leader in self-driving tech
	Aptiv—Software and sensors for autonomous vehicles
	Ambarella—Imaging processing and computer vision
3D printing and manufacturing	Proto Labs—Rapid manufacturing
	3D Systems—Maker of 3D printers
	Stratasys—Maker of 3D printers
	Materialise—Software for 3D printing

Extended reality—both virtual reality (VR) and augmented reality (AR)	Facebook—Own Oculus, a leading VR and AR company Microsoft—Focused on VR for business Sony—VR for gaming with Playstation Nintendo—maker of the world's #1 AR game, Pokemon Go!
Future of farming	Roots Sustainable Agricultural—Sustainable farming Deere & Company—Internet-enabled farming equipment Raven Industries—Maker of precision agriculture technology Origin Agritech—Seed breeding and genetically modified organisms

Doesn't the stock market crash?

There are famous stories of market crashes, but over time the stock market continues grinding upwards.

We've all heard the stories of market crashes—1929 Great Depression, 2008 Global Financial Crisis—there have been certain events when the markets have fallen and investors have lost money. Far less reported is the fact that the market has always recovered from these falls.

The reason the market recovers is that the companies that survive the downturn continue to get more productive, more innovative and more valuable over time. Individual companies will go bankrupt; technology will disrupt industries—but overall the market as a whole continues marching upwards.

Between 1900 and 2018, the Australian stock market had 23 years where it went down and 96 years where it went up: 81% of the years were good years.

It's not just that the stock market recovers from these crashes. Throughout history, time and time again, the stock market recovers from its fall and then keeps growing.

One of our favourite examples of this is the US stock market during the 2008 Global Financial Crisis. If you had invested in 2007, right before the market started falling:

- by February 2009 you would have lost half of your money and be feeling pretty ready to give up on investing

- by 2013, you would have been back to even (that would have been a long six years!)
- by 2019, you would have doubled your money.

Covid-19 made 2020 another tough year but it gave another example of the resilience of the stock market. If you had invested in Australia's market at the start of 2020:

- by 23 March, you would have lost one-third of your money
- by 24 November you would have been back to even.

Sure, it would've been a tough year. But the market recovered and then kept growing. As an investor, if you can hold your nerve during these stock market crashes, you'll be able to enjoy the recovery that comes after.

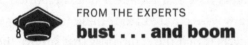

FROM THE EXPERTS
bust . . . and boom

In **Patrick O'Shaughnessy**'s book *Millennial Money* he explains how the market recovered despite two major crashes in the 2000s—the 2000 Tech Wreck and the 2008 Global Financial Crisis.

> '[In] the post-Clinton period between 1993 and 2011, the stock market grew by a real [after inflation] 162% . . . This post-1993 stock market growth happened despite two of the worst market crashes that we have ever seen, in 2000 and 2008, when the stock market twice declined more than 40%.'

Even with market crashes, over the long term the stock market has averaged up. You can see on the chart below how small the crashes look over the long term.

If you don't know what to make of these charts, don't worry. You don't need to understand charts to get started investing.

The US stock market over the past 100 years

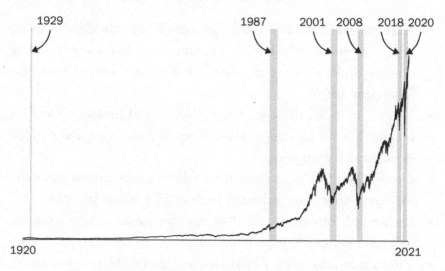

Here are the main things we've learnt over our journey at Equity Mates about stock market crashes:

- Stock market crashes will happen; they are a fact of life.
- Don't try to time the market and predict a crash; you miss out on gains and cause unnecessary stress.
- When a crash happens, the worst thing you can do is sell. It's too late and you'll often miss out on the recovery. Focus on the long term!
- Crashes have been great buying opportunities.

Our biggest takeaway? Markets have crashed and then recovered. They will continue to crash and recover. Fear of a crash shouldn't stop you investing because it'll stop you enjoying the awesome wealth-creating power of the market as well.

The market may recover but some companies won't

An important caveat to this is that individual companies can collapse and investors can lose money. While the overall stock market recovers, individual companies often don't.

There are some famous examples of companies collapsing in Australia.

- HIH Insurance: in 2001, Australia's second-largest insurer collapsed, losing investors over $5 billion. A number of senior leaders, including director Rodney Adler and CEO Ray Williams, went to prison for fraudulent activity.
- Qintex: in 1989, the company collapsed and investors lost $1.5 billion. The CEO, Christopher Skase, fled to Spain and avoided extradition for ten years.
- One.Tel: in 2001, the Australian telecommunications company collapsed, after being valued as high as $5.3 billion in 1999.
- Dick Smith Electronics: in 2016, the electronics retailer collapsed and investors lost $350 million.
- Virgin Australia: with Covid shutting down the travel industry in 2020, Virgin Australia was not able to continue operating and shareholders collectively lost close to $750 million.

Despite these famous examples of companies collapsing, the overall market continued growing higher. Many investors lost money on these companies, but investors who owned shares in a variety of companies recovered and saw their overall investments continue to grow.

The key takeaway here is that, when you invest, you shouldn't have all your eggs in one basket. This is a concept known as 'diversification', which we'll cover throughout *Get Started Investing*.

At this stage, all you need to keep in mind is that, while individual companies may be risky, the overall stock market is far less risky.

The reason is that, when you're investing in the whole stock market, you're investing in the productive capacity of the economy. Some companies will do well; some will do poorly. But overall the economy gets more productive, more innovative and, ultimately, more valuable.

It's FUN! How you view the world

Forget the idea that investing is about finance. It's about every aspect of the world around us.

Financial media does everyone a disservice when they make the stock market about charts, percentages and data points. Put all of that out of your mind.

When you invest in a company you are becoming a part-owner in that company. If you're going to invest in Nike, it's more important to know about sneakers than it is to know about financial charts.

In fact, if you look at the world around you, you'll realise you know a lot about the companies you could invest in: the shoes you wear, the phone you use, the car you drive, the shops you visit and the websites you browse. What trends are emerging, which ones are dying. What your friends and family talk about.

You'll start to realise you have far more insight into companies than charts or data could ever give you.

We're not just saying this. The expert investors we've interviewed on the podcast don't get all their information from charts and financial spreadsheets. They've shared some great stories of using the world around them to find stock ideas.

FROM THE EXPERTS
where to look for investing ideas

Julia Lee, the chief investment officer at Burman Invest, told us about how she used the world around her to research the Australian vitamin company Blackmores and their infant formula product. In particular, there were three things she looked at.

1 WHAT PEOPLE ARE BUYING

'When I go to the shopping centre or am looking at catalogues, there's a few things that I always check. One is if an area is seeing heavy discounting consistently. I also like to see what might be popular. During the baby formula stock boom, I would instinctively look at the baby formula shelves just to see what might be popular. And sometimes, you know, I stick around for a while and see what people are picking up and what they're looking at.'

2 WHAT CUSTOMERS ARE SAYING

'The other thing I do is check the review websites. Things like baby formula, if you've never had to use baby formula on a baby yourself, what you don't realise is that all baby formulas aren't the same. Some give certain babies constipation or runny poo. For a mother that's just had a baby, that's a fast reason to change baby formulas. Blackmores learnt this when it tried to launch a baby formula during the time when baby formula stocks were soaring. With food-based products, it's hard to simply cash in on a trend. There needs to be a good product as well. So I like to go to consumer websites, have a look at the reviews, I like to try and gauge what trends are in the market. I also ask the people around me. If they are mothers, what formulas they use and why. If they are millennials, I ask if they have a credit card, who they bank with and what buy-now-pay-later companies they use. Investing is about having an edge and sometimes asking the users of the products can give me an edge.'

3 WHAT IS BEING DISCOUNTED

'If I'm looking at catalogues, I'm trying to get a sense of where there might be increased discounting and hence a more difficult environment to grow profits. If it's vitamins and I see Swisse is discounting vitamins by 50%, I know that this would have an impact on demand for Blackmores and the margin it would be able to get for its products since Swisse is a major competitor in that space. The same goes with things such as travel, flights, insurance, phone plans. At the end of the day I'm trying to work out which areas have a declining market outlook due to more intense competition.'

Ed Cowan, former Australian cricketer and member of the investment team at TDM Growth Partners, explained how TDM is incredibly focused on finding businesses led by great people and with strong cultures.

'TDM's deepest belief is that "people and culture" is one of the strongest competitive advantages any business can have. We know that great people, with a shared mission and values, build wonderful, durable businesses for the long term.'

It can be hard to find out about the people and culture of a business. It certainly isn't something that is quantifiable like profit and it isn't explained in a company's annual report.

'It's kind of odd that you find yourself assessing people when you're not necessarily deemed an expert in the field, but it is easy to establish a basic sense of positive traits—a shared belief system, empathy, or modesty, fairly quickly. We also have a basic framework we use to diagnose culture that we have published on our website. For example, a red flag would be if a CEO uses the word "I" instead of "we", when describing company achievements. It suggests to us that they are not a team player and that as a leader, the culture he or she is building is not that of a high-performing team. Of the really big errors TDM has made, they have been errors in assessing the people. It is certainly probably the biggest decision that we make, and that is why we take so long to make it; we need time to make sure we get it right.'

He shared with us why people are so important when making investing decisions.

'At the end of the day, yes, we are investing in companies, but practically that means we are investing in the people to allocate capital on our behalf. When you own the business, any non-controlling share, you are backing the CEO, you're backing the board and you're backing the senior executives to grow these businesses over long periods of time. It is imperative that they are the right people to undertake this, and this is core to any investment decision we make.'

One resource that Ed uses to assess the leadership and culture of a company is a website, Glassdoor.com, which allows employees to leave reviews of the companies that they work for. Websites like this offer a great insight into the people and culture at a company, directly from the employees themselves.

Andrew Brown, executive director at East 72 Holdings, was interested in understanding the effect that ride-sharing app Uber would have on the Australian taxi market. So he went right to the source and signed up as an Uber driver!

'The first bit of real hard-nosed research I did was I drove Uber for three months. Now the reason I did that, it's all very well being an Uber customer. Okay, now we know Uber has undercut taxis and you could ride cheaply. So if you don't do the other side of the equation you just sit there and think Cabcharge is going out of business, because it's just discounted rides and you don't care . . . I wanted to see what it's like from the driver's point of view, because if Uber drivers make no money then Uber can't exist.'

After driving an Uber for three months, Andrew had some interesting insights on the Uber business.

'And the conclusion I came to was that, I knew very early on in the piece that the conclusion I came to was that it was quite clear if you drive Uber full time, you're not going to earn minimum wage. And you're certainly not going to earn minimum wage when you took into account the proper accounting of your time and your costs. And your costs, of course, are petrol. I can guarantee you'd have a much bigger chance of copping traffic fines and points and of course, the other thing is that you are wearing your car out at a much bigger rate of knots.'

We have all of this great information around us that we can use to understand the world and which companies are succeeding.

FROM THE EXPERTS
the power of common knowledge

Peter Lynch is a legendary American investor. As the manager of the Magellan Fund at Fidelity Investments between 1977 and 1990, Lynch consistently outperformed the American stock market by 100% (i.e. he doubled the growth of the US stock market year after year), making it the best performing fund in the world.

In his book *One up on Wall Street*, Lynch told the story of how a fireman found a successful investment from observing the world around him.

'There's a famous story about a fireman from New England. Apparently back in the 1950s he couldn't help noticing that a local Tambrands plant (then the company was called Tampax) was expanding at a furious pace. It occurred to him that they wouldn't be expanding so fast unless they were prospering, and on that assumption he and his family invested $2,000. Not only that, they put in another $2,000 each year for the next five years. By 1972 the fireman was a millionaire.'

What's more, Lynch explains how some of his best investments have come from observing the world around him.

'I talk to hundreds of companies a year and spend hour after hour in heady powwows with CEOs, financial analysts, and my colleagues in the mutual-fund business, but I stumble onto the big winners in extracurricular situations, the same way you would:

- Taco Bell—I was impressed with the burrito on a trip to California
- La Quinta Motor Inns—somebody at the rival Holiday Inn told me about it
- Volvo—my family and friends drive this car
- Apple Computer—my kids had one at home and then the systems manager bought several for the office
- Dunkin' Donuts—I loved the coffee.'

This is the great thing about investing in the stock market. Whatever aspect of the world interests you, there are ways to invest in that.

What's more, investing in the stock market allows you to be a more curious person. There are so many fascinating industries out there with interesting companies trying to solve big problems. Researching stocks is an avenue to learn more about them and deepen your understanding of the world in general.

So forget the spreadsheet and calculator. Think about what you're using, what you want your next big purchase to be. Speak to your friends and family about what they're spending more time on at the moment, what they're excited about, what they want to buy. Find industries and companies that pique your interest.

Investing doesn't need to be a dry, maths-based exercise. It should be an avenue for your curiosity.

The first step on your journey ... setting your investing goal

You've heard why everyone else invests. Now is the time to set an investing goal for you.

There's no wrong answer here. Everyone's investing goal is personal. The important thing is to have one.

Having an investing goal will help you stick with it. If it's as simple as to make money—great! If it's to stop you spending your pay on consumables—great! If it's to help you understand more about the world—that's great too! It doesn't matter what the investing goal is. The main thing is having a goal that motivates you.

We've shared a number of examples throughout this chapter. There are a number of common reasons—setting ourselves up for the future, not relying on a salary, providing a better life for our kids—but there are plenty of other reasons.

Everyone is different. Different family situations. Different life goals. Your investing goal needs to be personal to you. For a moment, focus on why you want to invest. Focus on what motivated you to pick up this book in the first place.

It helps to write it down. We've left some space for you to write your investing goal below.

What is your investing goal?

_____

_____

_____

_____

Section summary
YOUR PROGRESS

☑ WHY INVEST

At this point we hope you have a good understanding of why we invest and why you should too.

You have:
- ✓ discovered why other people in the Equity Mates community invest
- ✓ understood inflation and why not investing may be riskier than investing
- ✓ learnt about how the stock market is a compounding machine
- ✓ decided to stop relying on your pay and create other sources of income
- ✓ understood why we prefer the stock market over property
- ✓ created and written down your investing goals.

☐ BUILD AN INVESTOR MINDSET
☐ GET YOUR MONEY RIGHT
☐ UNDERSTANDING THE BASICS
☐ TAKING THE PLUNGE
☐ BEYOND THE FIRST INVESTMENT
☐ LESSONS WE WISH WE HAD KNOWN
☐ PULLING IT ALL TOGETHER

PART 3

Build an Investor Mindset

Investing is often put in the too-hard basket.
We want to change that mindset.

Change how you think about investing

Whether you're a twenty-year-old moving out of home for the first time or a little older with mortgage payments and kids to look after, we all have plenty of reasons not to invest. Not enough money, not enough time, not enough knowledge. The first step on your investing journey is to change your mindset. Challenging your beliefs and assumptions about investing and finding your reasons to invest make everything easier.

At times, we can be our own worst enemies. So many of our beliefs are formed when we're young and once they're set they can be very hard to shake. Our ideas about what we know and what we are capable of knowing are formed when we're growing up and then stick with us for life. For too many Australians, one of those beliefs is that 'investing isn't for me'.

The first thing we want to do is challenge that belief. Investing is for you.

If you don't believe us, that's okay. Just suspend your disbelief for the length of this book. Hopefully we can convince you by the end.

For too many Australians, we don't learn about finance and investing in school or from our parents, so we form assumptions about it.

- I don't have enough money to start investing.
- It is too hard to learn.

- Finance is too complex and time consuming.
- There's too much risk.

For the rest of the book, put all of that out of your mind. These are all myths that, along our journey, we've been able to bust.

Flip your mindset

You're not alone in thinking that investing isn't for you. There were times in the early stages of our journey that we even thought 'is this investing thing really for me?' A lot of the Equity Mates community also started in a similar place.

Do you want to know the good news? It's possible to flip that mindset.

We asked our community how their view of investing in stocks changed since they first started, and you can see they, too, have busted some of the investing myths.

Here are some of our favourite responses.

 FROM THE EQUITY MATES
community

We asked the community how their views on investing in stocks had changed since they first started investing. Among the many answers that came back, the biggest theme was that investing wasn't as hard as first thought and markets were easier to access than anticipated.

'Hugely. Initially, I thought stocks were exceptionally risky investments that were only viable for people with either a substantial amount of free time on their hands or people who worked in a related industry.'
ALEX

'I knew next to nothing. I couldn't even tell you what a stock was. I saw them as mysterious and dangerous. Now I am an active investor who makes an effort every single day to further my financial education.'
AMANDA

'I always felt that the industry was smarter and they had an edge. While most of the industry is very bright, they don't necessarily have an edge over single investors, temperament and behaviour trump any smarts in the long run.'

DAVID

'Less anxious. I began to see that investing small-sized amounts annually means that it doesn't matter if I mess up and buy stocks at a high price now and then. It all comes out in the wash.'

EMILY

'I always thought that you needed thousands of dollars to get started, but there are many options of micro investment platforms and resources like Equity Mates Podcast that one can use to learn about it and break all those paradigms.'

MAURICIO

'The share market is more accessible to the average person than I thought it was.'

MICHAEL

I don't know enough

At this point most investing books would throw a dictionary at you. Define every investing term from call option to candlestick. Explain the difference between a stock and a share.

Right now, we're not.

There's a lot of investing jargon that is used in the finance industry. For a lot of people, including us, that makes it really hard to understand what is going on. When we started the podcast there were still plenty of terms that we didn't understand. Lucky for us, we were willing to jump in anyway.

What we learnt from that experience is that you don't need to know everything up front. Learning as you go is the best way to learn about investing.

We're going to take that approach with *Get Started Investing*. At this stage, there is nothing you need to know. Nothing at all.

Throughout *Get Started Investing* we'll give you all the information you need to get started. We'll define key terms where appropriate but you can forget the idea that you need to understand every term and every aspect of investing right at the start.

For too many people this is a big reason that they never get started. The mountain of new terms and new concepts becomes too hard to climb. It is like learning a new language, starting out as a good idea before ending up in the too-hard basket.

Become a constant learner

We think of learning to invest as an ongoing process. Rather than building all your knowledge and then getting started, the best way to learn about investing is to build your experience and knowledge at the same time.

This is a difficult mindset change. In life, most of our learning comes before we get started. We do thirteen years at school before we are considered ready to go out in the world. It is the same sequencing for most jobs.

The normal learning sequence

Want to be a nurse:
At least two-year nursing degree ⎯⎯⎯⎯⎯⟶ Ready to be a nurse

Want to be an electrician:
Four years' study and apprenticeship ⎯⎯⎯⟶ Ready to be an electrician

Want to be a lawyer:
Five years of law school ⎯⎯⎯⎯⎯⎯⎯⟶ Ready to be a lawyer

Want to be a personal trainer:
At least six months to be certified ⎯⎯⎯⟶ Ready to be a PT

Want to be a commercial airline pilot:
Get 150 hours of flying time ⎯⎯⎯⎯⎯⟶ Ready for pilot's licence

It makes sense that when we decide to learn to invest, we approach it in the same way. We want to start by learning everything before actually taking the plunge and putting our money at risk.

For too many people, this is the decision that kills their investing dreams before they even get started. The stock market is a simple thing made incredibly complex by financial media and the investing industry. If you're going to spend a year reading financial news and investing books before you get started, I'd use Bryce's SportsBet account to bet you're more confused than when you started.

Think of investing this way—it is an easy thing to understand, and a hard thing to master.

If you are going to try to learn it through YouTube videos and books you're going to struggle to understand how this theory all works in practice. Instead, you need to learn as you go, having the practical experience to support your ongoing learning.

It may feel risky to get started before you know everything there is to know. You may feel like you're not ready. But it really is the best way to learn.

Over the course of this book we'll show you how you can start small, and we mean really small. Like a couple of cents or a few dollars small. Just dipping your toe in the water. As you grow in confidence and knowledge, you can move on to larger amounts of money.

At the end of the day, just like you learnt so much more in the first four months on the job than you did over four years at uni, there really is no comparison to learning by doing.

We've written *Get Started Investing* to introduce you to the key terms and concepts you need to understand to get started and we've made sure to exclude all the unnecessary detail. This isn't going to be a comprehensive guide to everything finance, and we definitely didn't write a Finance 101 textbook. This is your guide to getting started. To kick off your lifelong journey of investing.

Be an investor not a trader

The most important part of the investor mindset is to remain focused on the long term.

The stock market that we see in the media has warped our opinion of investing.

We are used to seeing fast-paced, short-term trading. Crowded trading floors with traders yelling orders over each other. Investors sitting at their desks in front of multiple screens, constantly buying and selling.

Forget all of that. That isn't investing.

Investing is a long-term game. It is difficult to make money trading day to day. You're competing with professional investors with better information, more experience and faster computers. More importantly, we all have better things to do with our time than sit in front of a computer screen for hours on end, watching prices move and staring at charts.

This introduces an important distinction that it took us a while to learn when we first started investing.

Are you an investor or trader?

In a lot of financial media, these two terms are used interchangeably. Trader or investor—either way you're buying and selling stocks, right?

That is correct. Both investors and traders buy and sell stocks. The key difference comes in the investing philosophy and time horizon.

Investors	Traders
• Look at the underlying fundamentals of a company	• Look at the price movement and short-term momentum and trends
• Think of themselves as part-owners of these businesses	• Don't worry about the long-term business fundamentals
• Hold investments for the long term	• Hold stocks for days or weeks at a time

There are plenty of ways to make money in the stock market. There's nothing wrong with being a trader. It just isn't for us, and we don't think it needs to be for most people.

As an investor, you're looking to become a part-owner of some of the greatest companies in the world—those companies that are hiring the smartest people, developing new products and services, and trying to solve some of the world's biggest problems. Investors want to find these companies and then hold them for a long period of time. At least years, but preferably decades.

Investors expect to make money by owning these shares and watching as the company grows its business, rolls out new products and services, and makes headway on these big problems. This isn't something that happens in a few days or weeks, but instead over a much longer period of time.

Forget 5 a.m. starts and hustle culture: getting rich may be for the lazy

Investors think about holding investments for a long period of time. While they're holding, there's not much they can do. Investors can't roll up their sleeves and help the business achieve its goals. We don't work for the company. Instead we watch and we wait.

Don't worry about early starts and hustling hard. The best investors can be lazy.

Investing is the opportunity to have your money work for you. As a part-owner of the company, there is nothing more to do than sit and relax.

Keep learning, keep up-to-date with your investments, keep researching new opportunities. But don't trade, don't watch the day-to-day movements of the share price, and don't try to draw shapes on charts.

Embrace the long-term investor mindset. You're not going to get rich quick. Investing is a lifelong journey.

WARREN BUFFETT
the investor mindset

Warren Buffett is the greatest investor in history. He is the CEO of Berkshire Hathaway and one of the wealthiest people in the world. Known for his simple investing philosophy (buy good companies and own them for a long time), when he speaks the investing world listens.

Buffett's philosophy is the best example of the 'investor' mentality. He isn't trying to trade stocks; he is trying to buy businesses.

> 'If you aren't thinking about owning a stock for ten years, don't even think about owning it for ten minutes.'

For Buffett, if he holds a fantastic business he doesn't even think about selling. He would be happy to hold fantastic businesses forever. We introduced some of the companies Buffett has owned earlier in this book: Coca-Cola since 1988, American Express since 1963 and Wells Fargo since 1989.

> 'When we own portions of outstanding businesses with outstanding managements, our favourite holding period is forever.'

Avoid the 'hot tip'

We've all been there. Whether it's at a family barbecue, at drinks with your mates or on social media, hearing about the 'next big stock' is tempting. Avoid them at all costs.

As much as we learn about long-term investing, the promise of a 'hot stock' or 'the next big thing' is tempting. When a friend tells you about a hot stock over a beer, it's hard not to follow their tip.

We're here to tell you to avoid that. A lot of the Equity Mates community have stories of following a mate's hot tip and regretting it later.

BRYCE'S
hot tip

I invested in a company called Shareroot, off the back of a hot tip from a mate of mine. It was a small company that specialised in providing a number of services in the social media space, from creating content for businesses to building marketing strategies.

My friend was pretty confident it could be the next big thing. To his credit, he'd done some due diligence, and even met with one of the management team. So I backed it in, without doing any research of my own. I really didn't understand too much about the company, other than at the time the share price was on a bit of a hot streak. I was sold the dream of a quick win! A couple of other mates also put a bit of their money in.

From day one, it went downhill. There were glimpses of its potential, but they struggled to execute their strategy, and the business never really seemed to take off.

The shares were sliding, but I held on for far too long. Perhaps with the hope they'd recover. Rookie! They eventually ended up suspending the shares, and changing their name, to pursue other business ideas. I ended up losing over 70%. When I finally sold, I mentioned it to my mate, and he said he'd sold ages ago! Thanks!

I may have lost some money, but I gained a lot of valuable lessons from the experience. I'm glad I learnt this lesson early, because since then, I've never taken a hot tip. You can't underestimate the value of knowing what you're investing in, and having your own thesis as to why.

FROM THE EQUITY MATES
community

Everyone has had that experience of the hot tip. We asked the community about some of their experiences with a hot tip and heard plenty of stories. Plenty of people have followed a hot tip; most people won't be following them again . . .

'My very first investment was actually because all my mates had just bought into a business with the ticker SAS. I knew nothing about it. I made about $200 and thought I was the king. (All my mates who didn't sell lost most of their money.) I took my proceeds and initial capital and put it into TLS on another "hot tip"—and proceeded to lose my $200. This was all in the space of three weeks. This taught me how quickly it can go well and how quickly it can go sour. And that hot tips and what your mates say are usually bullsh*t.'

JAAROD

'Terrible! A friend recommended a stock that I bought that is now down 40%. Wasn't a lot of money but definitely taught me a lesson to do your own research!!'

MEL

'Got a hot tip from my brother-in-law's brother and I possibly broke even on it. However the next tip turned into a disaster; I ended up placing two 15k orders by mistake and then the stock price crashed 95%.'

NATHAN

'Me and a friend (who is a nurse) decided to invest in VIP Gloves. He was very adamant about how well the company will do due to the demand for gloves in hospitals for Covid. Unfortunately I let his confidence in the business get the better of me. Long story short—I sold out at a 50% loss and this company is no longer ASX-listed. Lesson learnt: DYOR [do your own research] and never give in to your friends' tips so easily.'

PATRICK

'The second stock I bought was GXY, which I didn't really know/understand about. My then-boyfriend invested in it and he thought it'll be good because it's a lithium producer. And he said lithium would be needed especially with the up-and-coming electric cars. I was persuaded super easily. I think I might've bought when it was high and when it was growing rapidly? (Didn't understand the concept of "buy low" then!). Ended up losing half [my money]. I left it for I think two years before I sold it at a loss. Never buy stocks that I don't understand EVER AGAIN.'

SHARIN

'I had just sold my car and didn't know what to do with the money. A family friend told me about a mining company that was apparently going to triple in the next three months. I'm usually quite cautious but thought "what the hell" and bought $2,500 of this mining company. For the following weeks I was glued to my trading account constantly panicking at any sign of volatility. After six months of owning this miner enough was enough and I sold and lost probably 80% of what I put in.'

TRISTAN

At the end of the day, you need to always do your own research and come to your own decisions. Your friend won't be paying you back if you lose money following their hot tip.

And don't be that guy or girl telling your mates that your favourite stock is 'the next big thing' or 'guaranteed to go up'. There's nothing in it for you.

- If the tip goes well, you don't get any credit. It was expected. You were calling it 'the next big thing'.
- If the tip goes poorly, you're the person who lost your friend their money.

Section summary
YOUR PROGRESS

☑ WHY INVEST

☑ BUILD AN INVESTOR MINDSET

In this section we challenged the mindset a lot of Australians have when it comes to investing in the stock market. Forget the negative view, and focus on becoming a lifelong learner. Anyone can learn to invest and by the end of *Get Started Investing* you'll have the information and confidence to get started yourself.

You have:
- ✓ understood some of the negative beliefs Australians have about investing
- ✓ heard from the Equity Mates community about how they've changed these views since they started investing
- ✓ challenged the idea that you need to know everything about investing before you get started
- ✓ embraced the lifelong journey of learning to invest.

☐ GET YOUR MONEY RIGHT
☐ UNDERSTANDING THE BASICS
☐ TAKING THE PLUNGE
☐ BEYOND THE FIRST INVESTMENT
☐ LESSONS WE WISH WE HAD KNOWN
☐ PULLING IT ALL TOGETHER

PART 4

Get Your Money Right

The first step in your investing journey
is to get your money sorted.

I don't have enough money to invest

This is one of the most common reasons people don't start investing. With the cost of living always increasing, it is understandable. The good news is, with technology making markets more accessible than ever, you don't need a lot of money to get started.

Forget the idea that you don't have enough money to invest. Gone are our grandparents' days when you needed tens of thousands of dollars to get started. Gone are our parents' days when you needed thousands of dollars to get started. Thanks to technology, you can get started with as little as a few dollars and cents.

 LISTENER QUESTION
how much do I need to get started?

This is perhaps one of the most common questions we are asked. The simple answer is:

You only need a few cents. Literally. You don't need to be saving for years; you can be in the markets before you know it.

You may be asking, how is this possible?
Micro-investing to the rescue!

Micro-investing—turning cents into investments

Regardless of your income, or savings habits, there is a way to get into the market through **micro-investing**.

 PARDON THE JARGON
micro-investing

Micro-investing is a technological innovation that allows people to invest with incredibly small amounts of money. It pools everyone's tiny amounts of money and invests on behalf of this group in a range of investments.

Over time, if you put small amounts of money away regularly, it can grow into something much more sizeable.

Micro-investing is possible thanks to new technology and apps coming to the market. Traditionally you would need a minimum of $500 to start your investing journey but micro-investing apps allow you to invest cents. The best part? You don't need to know a lot about investing to use them!

Here's how. Micro-investing apps round up purchases you have made through your debit card, and invest the remaining spare change. For example, you buy a sandwich for $9.50. The micro-investing app will round it to $10 and take the $0.50 and invest it. Done! You're in the market!

Over time, as you make more purchases, your balance will slowly build and before you know you'll have a small nest egg invested in the markets.

Micro-investing apps generally have a number of investment options you can choose, from a conservative strategy to a high-growth strategy. They're a great way to understand how portfolios are constructed, and for you to dip your toe into the water without having to worry about choosing individual stocks and putting all of your hard-earned savings in right away.

Many members of the Equity Mates community have used micro-investing as their first step. These investments generally don't require a deposit to get started, they're convenient and very easy! You'll soon find that you understand more about how the market works purely by investing those small amounts of money. But more on this later. For now, forget the idea that you need a lot of money to get started.

FROM THE EQUITY MATES
community

We asked the community how they got started. Overall, 53% of the community we surveyed use a form of micro-investing. Many of them started small, with micro-investing apps.

'I used micro-investing through Raiz [one of the micro-investing apps in Australia, along with CommSec Pocket & Spaceship Voyager] to start off with and this really helped pique my interest.'
BEN

'I started small with micro-investing. Got comfortable with that, then began to invest in businesses that I knew!'
JAAROD

'I started with micro-investing . . . It was fine, cos it was so safe. I learned that to be safer, it's important to diversify and keep investing regularly (dollar-cost averaging).'
SHARIN

'I always thought that you needed thousands of dollars to get started, but there are many options of micro-investment platforms and resources like the Equity Mates podcast that one can use to learn about it and break all those paradigms.'
MAURICIO

'I initially started with RAIZ and this made saving fun.'
SIMON

'Having a micro-investing account has helped to invest spare change I may not normally save.'
SIMONE

Save to invest, don't save to save

Finding the money to get started can be tough. Even looking for a few dollars a month can sometimes seem insurmountable. We've faced the same challenges getting started. Here are a few tips and tricks we've learnt along the way.

If you're looking to bump up your investment amounts from a few cents to a few hundred or thousand dollars, then you're going to want to make sure your money-house is in order.

This doesn't mean you have to make radical changes to the way you live. Forget the idea that living a frugal life on baked beans is the only way to invest. Let's face it: money doesn't grow on trees. But, with a strategy and some discipline, you can make your money grow.

Saving can be tricky, especially when there are many other financial demands in life—your rent or mortgage payments, mobile phone bill, Netflix and Spotify, insurance, a night out. The list goes on. The good news is that it's still possible to invest without breaking your budget and living on two-minute noodles. All it takes is a plan and to start thinking about your savings differently.

Getting into the right savings habits can add fuel to your investing fire.

You want to be able to keep shovelling money into your investments. You want to be doing this as early as possible in your life to let compounding take effect. To do this, you need to be comfortable with putting money away specifically for investing every time you get paid.

It's so easy to look at your spare $100 at the end of the month and say 'Ah, but I may need this, so I'll just keep it in my account'. We've been there. Inevitably, it'll be spent.

If you can get into the habit of putting money away to invest, then your portfolio will be thanking you later in life. To do this, you need to actively think about saving to invest, not saving to save.

What do we mean by this?

Firstly, you need to separate money for saving and money for investing. All this means is consciously and actively putting some of your savings into another account that's used just to invest.

Let's say at the moment you are saving $500 a month. It's more than likely that money is going into a savings account, or just sitting in your spending account at the end of the month. You may have a saving goal, and that's awesome.

But as those savings grow, it's going to be harder to take money out to put in the markets. You'll likely feel worried about losing your hard-earned cash, or think 'But I might need this one day'. These are all valid emotions, and ones we've been through.

This is why it's important you start thinking about that $500 differently. At least some of it needs to be for investing, and investing only. An easy way to think about this is:

Saving to save =
putting money away for future use—a holiday, a car, a house

Saving to invest =
putting money aside that will earn a profit and grow

Secondly, any money you invest needs to be thought of as inaccessible. You don't want to touch it. Don't sell. Forget about it. There have been many times where we've had to do the cheeky transfer from our savings account to buy Christmas presents, or fund a holiday, or to splurge on some new clothes. The last thing you want to be doing is selling shares for activities like this. So, any money you invest, think to yourself 'this is not savings, it's my investment'.

Thirdly, never invest money you need. Don't blindly put money into the market when you know you have bills to pay or you're saving for a house deposit. You can't control the stock market, so putting money in that you need to live on or to buy something with in the short term is incredibly risky. Separate this spending money from your investing money, and keep it somewhere you can access when you need it.

 FROM THE EXPERTS
the benefit of starting small

Pete Matthew is a UK-based chartered financial planner and the managing director of Jacksons Wealth Management.

We asked Pete what advice he would give his younger self.

'I would say, start earlier. Start with small amounts. Even a small amount can compound. I would start earlier and commit to regular increases. That really is the magic. Starting at £50 a month, then committing in three months to make it 55 or 60. Then three months after that, make it 75. And just continually increase until it gets painful and then maybe hold for a bit, because before long, it won't be painful. You'll get used to it going out. And before you know it, the numbers get pretty exciting. So start early. Commit to regular increases and don't buy so much chocolate.'

Our tips on saving to invest

Everyone saves differently, and there is no right or wrong way to do it. All we encourage you to do is to find what works for you and stick with it. Consistency is key.

We both have different ways of saving to invest.

Bryce follows the 'Rule of Threes' principle. Simply, this is taking the money you earn and dividing it into three 'pots'. Let's say each fortnight you get $2,000. This can be divided three ways.

THE RULE OF THREES

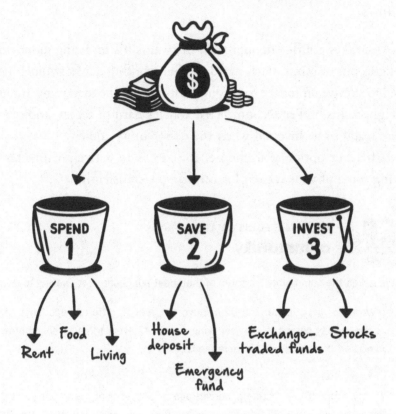

1 **Spending**—work out what you need to live. Rent, phone bills, gas and electricity, food, going out for dinner, Netflix, insurance, you name it. Ensure you firstly have enough for all the day-to-day expenses you will incur. This might be $1,300.

2 **Saving**—You now have $700 to save and invest. You might allocate $500 to a savings account for a rainy day, or for your next holiday, or your emergency fund. This is money you will want to access at some point.

3 **Investing**—you have $200 left, and as we mentioned earlier, this is money you now think of as your investing money. Money that

won't be accessed, and will be put away for a long time. Send this to another account if you need to. This is money you are saving to invest.

Alec takes a different approach. He wants his investing money out of sight, out of mind. Each pay day, after working out how much he'll need to survive on for the fortnight, he'll transfer the remaining amount straight to his broker account. That way it's hard to access, and sitting there ready to be invested when the opportunity comes.

Whatever option you choose, the key is to actively think about saving some of your money for investing. Consistently.

 FROM THE EQUITY MATES
community

We asked the community for some of their best suggestions for saving to invest.

'Work out living expenses then move the rest to different accounts as soon as pay comes in. Review living expenses every three to six months and see if savings can be increased.'
ALEX

'"Pay yourself first." Take a percentage or set amount from your pay as soon as you are paid and set it aside. Buy used cars, not new. Use an app to keep track of all of your spending and income to see where your money is going.'
ANYA K

'Assigning a percentage of your take-home pay to allocate to savings/ investing.'
ASHLEY

'Work towards short-term goals that actually matter to you. I struggled to save for savings' sake, but deciding I really wanted to open a Vanguard account gave me a goal of saving $5,000 that I wanted to achieve.'
CHRIS

'Do a budget and follow it, but never try to push your "investment" savings too far—something will always come up and get you disheartened if you can't reach your investment goal each month.'
DANIEL

'I am a spender, so it's seeing shares as a substitute for regular spending. So rather than spending $500 on a new gadget one month, I spend $500 on shares and that gives me the same spending kick.'
MICHAEL

Other tips to think about when getting your money sorted:

- Pay yourself first—automatically set aside some savings as soon as you're paid.
- Save for emergencies, keep it in cash.
- Spend less!
- Reduce discretionary spending habits—cut down on one UberEats per week, for example.
- Ask for help and guidance—there are professional financial planners who can set you on the right path.

FROM THE EXPERTS
little things do make a difference

Canna Campbell is the founder and director of SASS Financial Services, a financial planning firm. She is a financial commentator on Channel 9, founder of financial media platform SugarMamma.TV and best-selling author of *The $1000 Project* and *Mindful Money*.

Canna was able to invest $32,000 in one year, after doing whatever she could to save $1,000 at a time—called the '$1000 Project'. We asked her for some of her best savings tips, and ways to make extra money:

'On a personal note, with the $1000 Project, when I started this project, I had just gone through the end of a very painful, toxic and expensive divorce, and I had no money to invest myself. I was on such a tight budget to keep my own head above water and take care of my son.

Even if I wanted to have taken money out of my own salary or savings, that was actually not possible. First of all, I had to adjust my mindset because there's no point doing something like this if you don't really believe in yourself. That's why I just focused on the little things that you can do.

I focused on the $1,000 that I could save. I sat down and I went through my budget—little things, like I had Foxtel and I don't even watch television. So that immediately went. I learnt to take my lunch to work all the time, which then actually also had fantastic health benefits as well.

I learnt, you know, things like meal planning and food prepping to save money and reduce wastage—all these little things. Look at the way that you spend money.

Also, paying for things in cash because you're so much more present when you hand that $50 note over. I know I hate breaking notes and I have embraced the cashless society, but doing that cash exercise for such a long period of time, I'm so respectful of watching my account balance drop if I'm going to be swiping and tapping.

I also then look at ways you can stay within your existing lifestyle, but then also look at ways you can earn extra money, because it's the two different parallel worlds of saving and earning more. That's how you break your financial circumstances and raise your bar.

I enrolled in market research. I tested biscuits to washing powders, to washing machines, like all sorts of different things. And people thought I was completely nuts. And I was to a degree, but I was really passionate, determined to make this happen. And it was completely worth it.

So, what can you do? Can you walk dogs? Can you do some babysitting work? Can you do tuition? I have this one girl who was brilliant. She was actually a personal trainer, but she's also really good at carpentry. So she started to make life-sized [children's wooden play blocks] which she not only sells on Gumtree, but she also rents out to events and is doing really well.

Start doing things, thinking about ways you can earn extra money, like can you do cooking lessons? Can you cook people's meals to help them out? Can you do some nannying? What are the things you can do to help bring [in] some extra money? And these things really do make a huge difference.'

Sarah Hawley is an entrepreneur. We asked Sarah how she started her investing journey.

'I guess because I was working in the industry and learning all this stuff, I thought, well, I want to start investing myself. And I understood pretty quickly that it was a very important part of building wealth. You can't just save your money in cash, you have to actually invest in other assets ... Back then we didn't have as much access to some of the great new technology products we have now that kind of make the cost of investing a lot lower, but I think I saved up $1,000 or whatever it was that I needed to open an account and then started contributing in a monthly amount. And it was just like a diversified managed fund, probably had like four or five managed funds in that portfolio. And I just started, just went from there, put in whatever money I could afford every single month. If my pay would increase or whatever, top it up with a bit more. And that was how I started. So just a diversified portfolio.'

Investing while in debt

Should I be investing if I have a lot of other financial commitments, including debt? This is a common question we get and, in short, our answer is 'yes'. Why and how? We'll cover that in this next section.

Over the course of our investing journey we have both had debt. Be it government loans for study at university, loans through a bank, or even that nasty credit card, we've had to manage debt as part of our overall finances. The chances are that you too are paying off some form of debt.

One of the barriers you may be facing at the beginning of your investing journey is the conundrum between paying off debt and starting an investment portfolio. What should come first?

If deciding how much to save was tough, then prioritising what debt to pay, and what to invest in, can be even harder. Speaking from experience, the good news is that it is possible to service debt, and build a share portfolio.

But it is crucial you understand the type of debt you have, and the effect of **interest rates**.

 PARDON THE JARGON
interest rate

When you borrow money (think: for a mortgage to buy a house, or with your credit card) you pay interest on this debt. When you save money in the bank, the bank pays you interest on your savings.

The amount you get paid is determined by the **interest rate**. It is a percentage of the amount you've borrowed or saved.

For example, if you have $100 credit card debt, and the interest rate is 20% per year, you pay $20 interest every year on this debt. Alternatively, if you have saved $100 in the bank, and the interest rate is 3% per year, the bank pays you $3 for these savings.

Interest rate is always expressed as a percentage, and usually is an annual number (e.g. 20% interest usually means 20% per year).

Good debt, bad debt

Debt refers to borrowing money from another party, and is commonly used to buy large items, such as a car or a house. Another form of debt, and one that can be difficult to manage, is credit card debt.

Generally speaking you can look at debt in two ways. There's good debt, and there's bad debt.

Good debt is debt that you use to help build your wealth or improve your income. Examples of good debt would be a mortgage for your house. You're using the debt to buy your family home, which you hope will appreciate in value over time. Another good debt would be your student loan. You've used the money to study, and improve your chances of getting a job and earning a higher income. These types of debt generally have a relatively low interest rate, and can be paid off over a long period of time.

Bad debt is debt that does very little to help you build wealth and improve your financial position. The classic is a credit card or consumer loans. In most instances, these are used to buy consumables in the short term, and attract a relatively high interest rate.

Don't get us wrong. Sometimes you need to use a credit card to pay for a medical bill, pre-pay a holiday or even cover a round of drinks. Don't be hard on yourself if you do have some bad debt. You can get out of it.

The main thing is to be aware of the types of debt you have, as this will impact how you prioritise where your money goes.

The question becomes, how do you decide?

Broadly speaking, we believe getting rid of consumer (bad) debt as fast as possible is the best thing to do. There's no point having that nasty credit card debt sitting around.

If you want to be more technical, there is another way to think about it.

It comes down to interest rates.

Let's say you have some spare cash, and you're thinking about saving or investing it. You also have some money owing on your credit card. You need to consider the estimated return you will get from your investment, versus the interest you will have to pay on your credit card.

For example, if you invest your money into the stock market, you may expect to get approximately an 11% return on your investment in the first year. Great! As a side note: the reason you could assume this is that this is the average return from the stock market in Australia, over the last 40 years, not including franking.

But the interest you need to pay on your credit card may be 20%. In this instance, it is clearly best to put your money towards paying off your credit card before investing it.

Why? It's costing you more to have your credit card debt than the return you would get from your money in the markets. So pay down the credit card, and then turn your attention to investing.

 LISTENER QUESTION
I have $5,000: would it be better to pay off my credit card, or invest?

Let's assume the balance of the credit card is $5,000. Assuming the credit card interest rate is 20%, and the expected return on investment is 11%, we'll do the maths and have a look at what makes more sense.

Scenario 1: pay off the credit card. You may not earn anything from an investment that year, but you also won't have to pay any more interest.

Scenario 2: invest the $5,000. If you invest, you could expect a return of 11% that year, or $550. But you still need to pay 20% in interest for the credit card, which would be $1,000.

While you've made $550, you've also had to pay $1,000, leaving you $450 worse off than had you just paid off the credit card.

Let's look at another example with good debt. You may have a student loan that has an interest rate of 1.5%. If you invest your money into the stock market, you may expect to get an 8% return on your investment in the first year. In this instance, it makes sense to invest your spare money, and not worry about paying down your loan any faster.

Why? You're earning more money from the stock market than you're needing to pay on your student loan.

You can see in both examples it's important to consider how much interest you're paying versus your expected investment return. Our preference is to pay off bad debts as fast as possible, then focus on building wealth and steering clear of bad debts altogether. It's worth consulting a professional who can help determine the best approach for your situation.

 FROM THE EQUITY MATES
community

We asked the community how they thought about debt. Here are a few of our favourite answers.

'Don't get into debt young and start with even tiny regular amounts. If only I had known! Also, money is not a dirty subject. Talk to children and everyone else about it, if they are willing.'
KAR

'Pay off debt first before worrying about savings. Shop around for accounts with the lowest fees/best rates.'
MICHAEL

'Don't buy things you can't afford and don't buy things on credit. The only debt you should have is a mortgage.'
TREVOR

Do what feels right

Debt can also be a psychological hurdle—especially if you have multiple debts that you're trying to pay off. Having to then think about saving and investing can lead to feeling overwhelmed and not improving your financial position.

If you think it will make you feel better about your financial situation, feel like you've accomplished something, by clearing a debt or two—go for it. Don't be hard on yourself, but learn from the experience for next time. Clear the debt, celebrate the win and focus your attention on building that nest egg!

Just keep in mind that there is an opportunity cost to not investing early.

Bin that credit card!

There's no denying that credit cards can be enticing. Having the ability to pay for what you need or want, on the spot, if you don't have the cash, is an appealing offer. As enticing as they are, they can be a slippery slope.

If we haven't made it clear enough, credit cards are bad debt. They're not going to help you build wealth and should be avoided if possible when you're trying to start your investing journey.

If you do want a credit card, a good rule of thumb is:

- Ensure you have cash in your bank account to pay off the full balance at any time (e.g. you never go negative) and pay off the account every month.

- Never justify a negative balance by thinking 'I have a pay cheque coming in soon that will cover this month'. Your spending is getting ahead of your financial situation and you need to rein it in.

There are alternatives to credit cards that don't incur the high interest rates.

Buy-now-pay-later (BNPL) companies are becoming popular. These companies allow you to purchase a product on credit, and then pay it off over a specific period of time. Generally, there is low, or no, interest charged on the purchase.

The service is offered by the retailer when you purchase an item at checkout. Rather than pay with your debit card, you can select to pay via one of the BNPL companies, which pays the retailer on your behalf. Over a set period of time—such as four regular instalments—you pay the cost back to the BNPL company.

The advantage here is you have a longer interest-free period compared to credit cards and the BNPL companies direct debit the money from your account. No remembering to pay off your credit card at the end of every month. Examples of companies in Australia that offer this service are Afterpay, ZipPay and Humm.

Earning more money? Avoid lifestyle creep

It feels great to be given a pay rise, or a bonus, or to earn some extra cash on the side. The key is to put that money to work for you over the long term and to avoid the temptations of the short term.

Let's face it. We all want to earn more money, as soon as we can. We want to earn more so we can improve our standard of living. There is nothing wrong with that.

You may have just received a pay rise—congratulations! You may be lucky enough to have been given a bonus. You may be earning some extra cash from a side hustle. All of these examples have put extra cash into your back pocket, and more than likely it has improved your **discretionary income**.

 PARDON THE JARGON
discretionary income

The portion of your income that is left to spend, save or invest. For example, you earn $2,000 a fortnight. After taxes, and living expenses, you have $500 left to do what you want. That is your **discretionary income**.

As your discretionary income improves, the more spare cash you have and the more tempting it is going to become to splurge more often. This is called lifestyle creep.

Lifestyle creep is where spending on non-essential items increases as your standard of living improves, or in other words, as you earn more money. Where you once thought a service or item was a 'want', it now becomes a necessity. Don't get us wrong, there's nothing wrong with rewarding yourself with something nice when you earn a little more cash or get that bonus.

The key is to ensure it doesn't become a regular habit. If you start to spend more consistently on non-essential services and items, you will reset your 'baseline'—your base cost of living. The risk in doing this is that if you were to unfortunately start earning less, or you lose your job, then you're going to need to dip into savings to maintain your standard of living.

Remember, you want to be putting money into investments as early as you can, and as much as you can. Take advantage of that wonderful thing called compounding. One way you can do this is to avoid lifestyle creep and funnel your discretionary income into your investments.

Avoid lifestyle creep and boost your investments

There are four simple ways you can try to avoid lifestyle creep and put that extra hard-earned cash into investments that will build your wealth.

1 Don't change anything, keep your baseline! Sit on your extra cash for a little bit. Don't rush into getting a new house with higher rent. Avoid subscribing to those three extra streaming services. Stay with your local restaurant and refrain from the fancy ones. We're not saying don't enjoy life. Just keep doing what you were doing for a while.
2 Stick to your budget and redistribute your spare cash. What do we mean by this? Tip number one was to keep your baseline spending the same. Now the best thing you could do is redistribute your extra cash. If you're getting an extra $500 per fortnight, try to put as much as you can into your saving and investing pots. The

extra money will add up quickly over time. Your future self will thank you!

3 Automate your saving and investments. To make it easier to put that extra cash away, have it out of sight and out of mind. Set up direct debits the day you get paid, transferring the cash to your savings and investment accounts. This way you're less likely to be tempted to splurge.

4 Slowly make change. Of course, if you get the pay rise, there's probably an urge to upgrade your headphones or buy a new couch. Try to focus on the things that will make a big difference in your life, and avoid the temptation of short-term shiny new things!

AVOID LIFESTYLE CREEP

Think about your future you!

Investing is all about putting money away now for a better tomorrow. Resisting the impulse for immediate satisfaction knowing it will result in greater satisfaction in the future is known as delayed gratification.

If you are fortunate enough to have some spare cash, no debt to pay off and you're faced with the dilemma of buying a new TV or putting it into the markets, think about your future you! You're much more likely to be stoked with a sizeable portfolio in 20 years than the new TV you bought.

FROM THE EXPERTS
what to do with extra income

Pete Matthew is a UK-based financial planner and the managing director of Jacksons Wealth Management. When we spoke to him, this was his comment about what to do with extra income.

'The key to becoming wealthy all the time is to make sure you capture any increases in your income or any windfalls that come. If you get promoted and you get an extra, I don't know, 200 bucks a month coming in, you've got to say, "Right, what am I going to do with that? Am I going to just let my lifestyle increase, go out to eat a couple more times, maybe ramp up my Netflix subscription or whatever? Or am I going to put that money to good use?" I will be saying, "Right, I'm going to enjoy 50 bucks of that extra, the other 150 I'm going to pay my mortgage. I'm going to increase my pension savings or whatever".

Be intentional. Nobody got wealthy by drifting. No Olympic athlete ever fell out of bed and onto the podium. We need to be intentional with every single decision we make around money.'

Section summary
YOUR PROGRESS

☑ GET YOUR MONEY RIGHT

It's time to dispel the myths you've heard about needing a lot of money to invest. You can get started with as little as a few cents. With the right strategy, and some discipline, you can start to think about your savings differently. Don't save to save, save to invest. Make sure you review any debt you have, and pay off that nasty stuff first! And remember—avoid that lifestyle creep!

You have:
- ✓ stopped telling yourself you don't have enough money to start investing
- ✓ signed up to a micro-investing app
- ✓ set up a savings system that helps you save to invest
- ✓ reviewed any debt you have—is it good or bad?
- ✓ binned your credit card!
- ✓ saved and invested any extra money you've earned—avoiding lifestyle creep.

PART 5

Understanding the Basics

Welcome to the world of investing.

You don't need to know everything

Just a reminder that you don't need to know everything, but here are some things to get you started.

Let's take stock: what is a share?

First things first: what is a share? Or a stock?
Basically, what am I buying?

To understand a stock, it helps to think about a basic company you are familiar with. Maybe it's a local cafe or your favourite pub. Cut out all of the noise and complexity of the stock market and just start with a simple-to-understand business.

You start a pizza restaurant with your best friend. You each want to own half the restaurant—how do you set that up?

You set up a company and create two ownership shares for the company: one goes to you and the other to your friend. Given there are only two ownership shares, each share owns half the company.

For a while you run the cafe and things are going well. You decide you want to open up a second location. You know you make the best pizzas in town, you just don't have the money for a down payment and fit-out of the second location. To do this, you need an investor to put some money in.

In return, the investor wants an ownership share of the business. So you and your friend, as the owners of the two shares in the company issue a third share and sell it to the investor in return for their money. Now there are three shares, with three different owners, meaning each person owns one-third of the (now larger) business.

A share is simply an ownership stake in a business. Some companies may only have one share. Others have billions. However many shares a company has, the owners of these shares are together the owners of the business.

is there a difference between a share and a stock?

This is a common question, and with good reason. You hear people talk about 'owning stock' and also 'owning shares'. Similarly, people seem to use the terms 'stock market' and 'share market' interchangeably.

The good news is that these terms are used interchangeably to refer to an ownership stake in a company. An owner of a share or an owner of stock is a part-owner of a company.

While there are some historical and technical differences, you can lead a long and happy investing life without ever worrying about the difference.

For all intents and purposes, stocks and shares refer to the same thing.

If you really want to understand the technical difference, 'stock' is a more generic term that describes a slice of ownership of one or more companies, whereas 'share' is a more specific term that refers to the ownership of a particular company.

Technically, a person explaining in general terms that they own investments would use the term 'stocks'. If that person goes on to explain that they own shares in Commonwealth Bank, they would be using 'shares' correctly.

In reality, the terms are used interchangeably.

If you want more information on this difference, we suggest googling 'Investopedia stocks versus shares'.

So what is the stock market?

The stock market (aka the share market) is where ownership stakes in businesses are traded. Those who own shares in businesses can sell their shares to people wanting to buy stakes.

Let's build on our pizza restaurant example. Let's say our investor wanted to sell their share in the pizza business. They could do that without the stock market. They'd just have to find a willing buyer.

They'd have to start calling people they know, maybe put ads online, trying to find someone interested in buying a share in a thriving pizza restaurant. Then they'd have to negotiate a price for that share and then draw up all the legal documents to actually make that sale.

The stock market automates all of this.

If our pizza restaurant was listed on the stock market, then the investor could enter into the market and say they want to sell. If anyone has entered into the market and said they want to buy a share in the restaurant, then those orders would be matched and the sale would be made.

At the end of the day, that is all the stock market is. A place where owners of businesses can sell their stakes in those businesses. It is a place where people who want to own businesses can go and buy stakes in businesses.

How does a company get listed on the stock market?

When a company decides to get listed on a stock market, it goes through a process of changing from a **private company** to a **public company**.

PARDON THE JARGON
private and public companies

Private companies (aka listed companies) are companies that are not listed on a stock exchange. The majority of companies in Australia are private companies, and each is owned by a small group of shareholders. These companies have to report their sales and profit to the Tax Office but do not have to report these results publicly.

Public companies are companies that are listed on a stock exchange. These companies are owned by a much larger group of shareholders and have to report their sales and profit to the public.

The actual mechanics of this process is simply our pizza restaurant example on steroids. In our pizza example, we were looking for one investor and issued one share to sell to the investor. When a company gets listed on the stock market, they sell millions or billions of shares in return for millions or billions of dollars.

The company gets this money to continue to grow its business and these investors are able to sell their investment in the company whenever they want on the stock market.

What are you actually buying?

When buying a share, you are becoming a part-owner of a business.

That is the most important thing to keep in mind. It isn't just a code on a computer screen or a piece of paper you keep filed away in a drawer. You are a part-owner of the business.

How much of the business you own depends on how many shares the company has issued. Think of it like a pizza.

To start with, our pizza parlour had two owners, so each owned half the business

When more investors came in, the business became even bigger but was split ten ways

When an investor came in, the business became bigger but each share was one-third

YOUR SLICE OF THE BUSINESS

A company can issue as many or as few shares as it wants. Most companies that you can buy on the stock market have been broken up into millions or billions of shares. If you bought a share of a company with 1 million shares, then that one share would mean you own 0.0001% (one-millionth) of the company.

Here are the most and least number of shares issued in Australia's 200 biggest companies (as of February 2021; this will change as companies issue more shares or buy them back).

Most shares	Telstra	11.9 billion shares
Least shares	Blackmores	19.1 million shares

What does it mean when you own a share?

So you own a share. Congratulations, you are a part-owner of a company. What does that mean?

As a part-owner of the company, you are entitled to:

* get paid some of the company's profits
* participate in the decisions of the company
* vote for who becomes members of the company's board.

Markets

Almost every country in the world has a stock market and, with the internet, all of these stock markets are now more accessible than ever.

In the previous section we introduced the concept of a stock (share) market: a place where people who are business owners can sell their shares in a business and where other people can become part-owners of businesses.

Australia has three stock markets—the Australian Securities Exchange (ASX), the National Stock Exchange of Australia (NSX) and Chi-X Australia (CXA). The ASX is by far the biggest and has most of the companies you've heard of—Commonwealth Bank, Woolworths, Telstra etc.

How does a stock market actually work?

Stock markets are places where people meet to buy and sell shares of businesses. They also publish the price that these shares are sold for, so anyone can see what they would need to pay for a share of a business.

Back in the day, people met in physical locations to buy and sell shares. Think those trading floors you see in movies and TV shows. These days, almost all shares are traded over the internet.

INVESTING THEN
—— VS ——
INVESTING NOW

Trading floor   Online trading system

People who want to buy shares place orders with the stock market, saying what they want to buy and what they're willing to pay. At the same time, people who want to sell shares tell the stock market what they want to sell and at what price they're willing to sell it.

The stock market's job is to match these buy orders and sell orders.

If a buyer tells the stock market they want to buy a share of Woolworths for $40 and a seller tells the stock market they are willing to sell a share of Woolworths at $40, the stock market will connect these two and facilitate that trade.

⁇⁇ LISTENER QUESTION
how is a share price set?

In the news every evening, we hear reports about how share prices have moved. Woolworths up 10%, Telstra down 2%, Afterpay down 15%. It can be confusing to know how these prices are set and why they move so much.

The share price that we see and that gets reported in the news is simply the last price a share was sold at. The way the share price moves throughout the day is simply the price at which a buyer is willing to buy and a seller is willing to sell. It is the last price at which a share is sold.

The reason share prices move so much throughout the day is that there are so many buyers and sellers. Every day there are millions of shares that are bought and sold. Because there are so many people trading, the price is constantly moving.

What are some of the major stock markets around the world?

There are 60 major stock markets in the world. They range from America's largest stock market—the New York Stock Exchange, representing $18.5 trillion—to the world's smallest stock markets—Malta, Cyprus and Bermuda, which represent between $1 billion and $4 billion. Sixteen of these stock markets represent more than $1 trillion. Don't worry, you don't need to know them all. Here are a few of the world's major stock markets that you may come across.

- Australia: Australian Securities Exchange
- Canada: Toronto Stock Exchange
- China: Shanghai Stock Exchange and Shenzhen Stock Exchange
- European Union: Euronext
- Germany: Deutsche Borse
- Hong Kong: Stock Exchange of Hong Kong
- India: Bombay Stock Exchange and National Stock Exchange
- Japan: Japan Exchange Group
- New Zealand: New Zealand Stock Exchange

- South Africa: Johannesburg Stock Exchange
- United Kingdom: London Stock Exchange
- United States of America: New York Stock Exchange and National Association of Securities Dealers Automated Quotations (NASDAQ) Exchange.

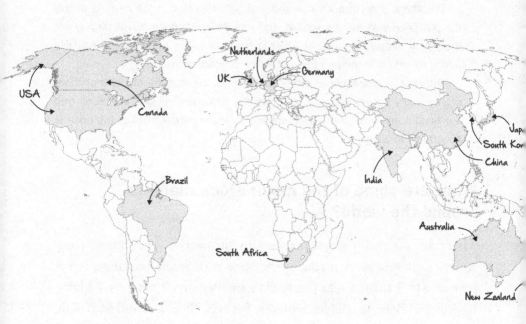

Index

We've introduced the concept of a share and the markets where shares are traded. The next concept to understand is an index— a basket of stocks that measures the movement of a market as a whole.

Have you ever heard the financial news say 'the stock market was up today' or 'the stock market didn't react well to that news'?

As we've just explained, the stock market is made up of thousands of individual stocks—so how can we talk about the 'stock market' as a whole?

To measure the stock market as a whole, we use the concept of an **index**.

 PARDON THE JARGON
index

An **index** measures the change in prices across a group of stocks over time.

It follows the sum of all of the stocks in the group. Every day, some go up and some do down in price; the index tracks the overall movement of these stocks together.

An index usually tracks the largest stocks in a particular stock market or a particular industry or segment of a market.

Why are indexes important?

A fair question at this point is: so what? As everyday investors we've got better things to do than worry about what the market is doing day to day.

The reason that indexes are important is that they allow us to invest in a bit of everything. Rather than picking an individual stock, we can put our money with the whole market or a particular industry. We'll explain how you do this later in *Get Started Investing*. At this stage, just keep in mind that indexes are an option for you to invest in.

How do we understand indexes?

To illustrate the concept of an index, let's use everyday things that we own instead of stocks.

Let's say we own three assets—a car, a house and a watch. We know what we paid when we bought them.

What we own	What we paid
Apartment	$500,000
Car	$10,000
Watch	$1,000

If we go and get these assets valued, we now know what they're worth and can measure how they've changed.

What we own	What we paid	What they're worth	Change
Apartment	$500,000	$550,000	+ $50,000 (Up 10%)
Car	$10,000	$8,000	– $2,000 (Down 20%)
Watch	$1,000	$950	– $50 (Down 5%)

The question then becomes: how do you value all of these three things together?

This is where the concept of indexing comes in. If you add up their cost and then measure their change in price together, you are measuring them as a group. This is an index.

What we own	What we paid	What they're worth	Change
Car, apartment and watch together	$511,000	$558,950	+ $47,950 (up 9.38%)

Applying this to the stock market

This concept of combining all the different assets is how a stock market index works. By combining the price of all the different shares and then measuring the overall movement of them all combined, we can measure how the market moves as a whole.

To give an example, we're going to use the big six technology stocks—Facebook, Apple, Amazon, Netflix, Alphabet (which is Google) and Microsoft. Let's say we wanted to measure the change of these six stocks from 2015 to 2019. We can index these stocks and measure them as a group.

Stocks	Market value in 2015 (billions)	Market value in 2019 (billions)	Change
Facebook	$218	$594	+ $376 (+ 172%)
Apple	$633	$1,279	+ $646 (+ 102%)
Amazon	$143	$924	+ $780 (+ 544%)
Netflix	$21	$144	+ $123 (+ 582%)
Alphabet (aka Google)	$361	$938	+ $578 (+ 160%)
Microsoft	$382	$1,211	+ $830 (+ 217%)
Together (as an index)	**$1,759**	**$5,091**	+ $3,332 (+ 189%)

If these amounts don't quite add up, it's because some numbers have been rounded off.

Some notable indexes from around the world

Every major stock market in the world has an index. It is the primary way investors track the movement of an overall market (i.e. you may have heard in the news 'Australia's market was up 2% today'). Here are some of the major indexes around the world.

- Australia: the ASX 200 follows the largest 200 Australian stocks; the All Ordinaries follows the largest 500 Australian stocks
- Canada: TSX Composite Index follows the largest 250 Canadian stocks
- China: SSE Composite Index follows all stocks listed on the Shanghai Stock Exchange; SZSE Component Index follows the largest 500 stocks traded on the Shenzhen Stock Exchange
- European Union: Euronext 100 follows the largest 100 stocks traded on the pan-European Euronext stock exchange
- France: CAC 40 follows the largest 40 French stocks on the Euronext Stock Exchange
- Germany: DAX 30 follows the largest 30 stocks on the Frankfurt Stock exchange
- India: Sensex follows 30 shares listed on the Bombay Stock Exchange; CNX Nifty follows 50 shares listed on the Indian National Stock Exchange
- Japan: Nikkei 225 follows the 225 largest Japanese stocks
- New Zealand: NZX 50 follows the largest 50 stocks on the New Zealand Stock Exchange
- South Africa: JSE 40 follows the largest 40 stocks on the Johannesburg Stock Exchange
- United Kingdom: FTSE 100 follows the largest 100 British stocks
- United States of America: Dow Jones Industrial Average follows a group of 30 selected American stocks; S&P 500 follows the largest 500 American stocks; the NASDAQ 100 follows the largest 100 stocks traded on the NASDAQ stock exchange

Other types of indexes

Indexes are used to track more than just the overall market. They can also be used to track different themes or segments of the market. Here are a few notable examples in Australia and around the world and what they track.

- ASX All Technology Index: tracks the share price performance of all Australian technology companies listed on the Australian stock market
- Australian Financials Sector: tracks the share price performance of Australia's biggest financial companies, including banks like Commonwealth Bank and National Australia Bank and insurance companies like QBE and Suncorp Group
- Australian Resources Sector Index: tracks the share price performance of the largest Australian resource companies, including oil and gas companies such as Woodside Petroleum and Santos, and mining companies such as BHP and Rio Tinto
- Future Australian Sustainability Leaders Index: tracks a group of Australian companies that do not have significant exposure to fossil fuels and are not engaged in activities deemed inconsistent with ethical investment considerations
- Global Agribusiness: tracks the share price performance of the world's largest businesses in the agriculture sector
- Global Railway Performance Index: tracks the share price performance of the world's twenty largest international railway companies
- Global Video Gaming and eSports Index: tracks the performance of the global video gaming industry, from those companies that develop games, software and hardware to those offering streaming services and those involved in eSports events
- Global Waste Management Index: tracks the share price performance of the world's 25 largest waste management companies, including Australia's Cleanaway and Sims, America's Waste Management and France's Suez and Veolia.

Investing styles

At this stage you understand some of the key 'whats'—what a share is, what a stock market is and what an index is. Now we want to get into the 'how' and explain how you can invest.

There's no perfect way to invest.

That's how we want to start this section. There are plenty of ways to make money in the stock market. Different strategies, different styles, different philosophies. There's nothing wrong with that but it can get confusing. It's easy to get lost trying to figure out how all the experts have made their money and how to follow them.

In this section we want to introduce you to the different styles of investing. These styles all look at different things and have different time horizons.

There's no right way to invest. The most important thing is to think about what style makes sense to you.

Most investors take the best bits from all of these styles and combine it into something that works for them. Your preferred style will also change over time, so don't worry if you don't know what style of investing makes sense for you at the moment.

The different styles of investing

	Value investing	Growth investing	Passive investing	Momentum trading
STRATEGY	Looks for stocks that are 'cheap'.	Looks for stocks that will grow quickly.	Focuses on buying and holding indexes and then not doing anything.	Makes money from short-term changes in share price.

	Value investing	Growth investing	Passive investing	Momentum trading
HOW IT WORKS	Investors figure out what they think a share should be worth (this is known as intrinsic value) and then buy the share if it is cheaper than what they think it is worth.	Investors are looking for companies that have great business prospects and will grow their sales and profit a lot over the next few years.	Historically, the Australian stock market has averaged 9% return a year. Many investors are happy to take this return, so invest in market indexes that give them market average returns.	Every day a company's share price is constantly moving, as thousands or millions of shares change hands. Traders look for companies that have growing share prices and ride this momentum up. They don't look to hold for the long term, maybe only for days or weeks, and then they sell when the momentum slows down.
WHAT INVESTORS LOOK AT	The fundamentals of a company: how much profit it makes and how much money it has.	Metrics like how quickly sales and profit are growing.	Almost no research, because investors just buy index funds that track the whole market, meaning no research on individual companies or trying to forecast how companies will grow into the future.	Charts and data on how many people are buying or selling a stock.
WHO'S IT FOR?	Investors willing to spend the time analysing individual companies and looking at their financials.	Investors interested in looking at growing industries and the companies that are 'winning' in these industries.	Investors who are time poor or not interested in spending a lot of time on their investments. It is a true 'set and forget' style of investing.	Investors who can spend a lot of the working day following the market and are able to make quick buy and sell decisions.

How we invest at Equity Mates

ALEC

My preferred investing style is a combination of growth and value investing. Since I started investing, I've seen some phenomenal companies grow into some of the biggest in the world. Microsoft, Amazon, Apple—investors who owned stocks in these companies have seen some incredible results.

For me, the biggest opportunity in investing is to find the next big growth stocks, the companies that develop exciting new technology or help solve a big problem like climate change. That's what gets me interested in investing and what I love researching.

At the same time, the more investing books I've read, the more I have learnt how many of these 'growth companies' are very expensive. Investors have a lot of expectations for these companies so they're willing to overpay. I try to incorporate some of the lessons of value investing to ensure I don't pay more than I should for a stock.

BRYCE

Gut feel.

Seriously, though, I have two investing styles.

The first is passive. I have a core portfolio of exchange-traded funds (ETFs), covering many markets around the world, and a number of different asset classes. I buy into these ETFs at regular intervals, with the same amount of money each time. This is dollar-cost-averaging. I have no intention to sell these in the short term.

My second approach is similar to Alec: growth investing. I'm looking for companies that are on the edge of their industry, trying to break new ground or even creating entirely new markets. I'm looking for companies that have a dominant position in their industry, or will be really hard to compete against. Then, I back them in and enjoy the ride!

FROM THE EXPERTS
how the experts invest

Rory Lucas is chief investment officer of Hearts & Minds Investments Ltd.

'Most of my career has been trading equities . . . it's about trying to find undervalued and overvalued stocks. Generally, I'd hold positions anywhere from two days to three or four months—however long it took to no longer be under- or overvalued—unless of course new information changed my thesis, causing me to cut and run quickly.'

Tobias Carlisle is founder and managing director of Acquirers Funds LLC, serving as the portfolio manager for their deep-value strategy.

'What I'm looking for is something that's just deeply undervalued . . . deep value is sort-of not so much caring about the quality of the business, looking more for the undervaluation. It's not that I don't care about the quality of the business, it's just that I have a different definition of quality. And my definition of quality is a cash-rich balance sheet, accounting earnings that turn into cash flows and management that's taking advantage of the undervaluation by buying back stock or doing something else that enhances value. And I find that those things together do very well.'

Pete Matthew is a UK-based chartered financial planner and managing director of Jacksons Wealth Management.

'I think when it comes to investing I am an inherently lazy person . . . What I preach on the show really is a very hands-off method of investing. That's not to say that there isn't a place for more active investment if that's an interest of yours. But it really isn't of mine, ironically. I tend to preach passive multi-asset investing. There's two parts to that, of course, passive means we're tracking markets rather than choosing individual stocks . . . Multi-asset simply means really diversified across different kinds of assets and across different geographical locations.'

Julia Lee is the chief investment officer of Burman Invest.

'I definitely like bargains but not just for bargains' sake. I prefer growth at the moment, whether it's earnings growth, price growth or user growth. I tend to adjust my strategy depending on what's happening in the global economy. I believe that most things move in cycles, including the stock market, and that different strategies perform better at different times in that cycle. The last thing I'd want to be doing is increasing exposure to growth-focused companies when an economy is about to head into a recession or vice versa. I try to keep in mind what's happening in the cycle to understand whether I should be more cautious or taking more risks.'

Chris Reining is an everyday investor who retired at 37.

'[M]y strategy was to continually put money into an index fund and also build a small stock portfolio.'

Brandon van der Kolk is the founder of New Money.

'For me personally, investing in what I know is a crucial part of the way that I invest. Because I find that if I start looking at things that I don't really know much about, I stray outside my circle of competence, the likelihood that I make a bad investment is going to go up . . . I definitely invest in things that I really like. Like companies for instance, I'll get Facebook. I use Facebook every day; I know the ins and outs of Facebook, so it's going to be much easier for me to understand Facebook as a company than banks.'

Andrew Page is the founder and managing director of Strawman.com.

'I definitely have an investment philosophy. And I think it's probably best stated as good businesses at good prices held for the long term.'

Tom Piotrowski is an economist and market analyst for CommSec.

'The best investment philosophy is one where you take a long-term view, because under those circumstances, what you're able to do with the benefit of that time frame is you can insure yourself or inoculate yourself against the inherent volatility of markets and price movements. Then you are able to focus on fundamentals like the quality of an organisation through its management, the people who make up the intellectual property of the organisation, the ideas that they have, the systems that they have that the organisation is based on. And then it just comes down to the very simple idea of after you've paid the bills that are associated with running your business, how much money do you have left over which you can either reinvest into your business or return to your investors? It sounds quite simple, but it is a challenge when you go into a stock market and try to pick apart all of these businesses. But it is the best and proven approach to making money over the long term when it comes to investing in companies.'

Nick Griffin is the chief investment officer at Munro Partners.

'When you're investing in an equity, you're generally investing in someone's vision. Someone's idea. That could be truly great or it could fail spectacularly. And the key thing to remember is the vast majority fail spectacularly . . . But what's interesting about it is there are always only a few winners. Right. Thousands of companies tried to build a plane, but there's only two companies that can build a plane that you and I will knowingly get on: Airbus and Boeing. And so once you understand that is your philosophy, you realise that equity investing is actually about just going out and trying to find these exceptional companies.'

Emilie O'Neill is an equities analyst at eInvest/Perennial Value Management.

'I think if you're not a professional investor and you don't have enough funds to diversify your portfolio, you should really be looking at managed funds and ETFs, which is a great way to kind of get exposure to different geographies and different sectors and have it managed by professionals—so my investment philosophy and what I tell my friends is, if you don't have the time and you don't have the funds, look at one of those options because they're going to give you better outcomes longer term.'

Rudi Filapek-Vandyck is the founder and editor of FNArena.

'I've actually learnt by doing this that quality is, in the end, what gets you through times, through tough times and the good times . . . But my research has led me to re-emphasising and actually really, really focusing on quality. In a world wherein everyone is focused on price or valuation, quality is the most underrated characteristic for an investment in the share market.'

Nick Cregan is a portfolio manager at Fairlight Asset Management.

'We love businesses that generate lots of cash, so we loosely defined those businesses as quality companies . . . And then we employ, as I mentioned, three slightly different styles of investing within quality. So we've got growth. We've got what we call stable compounders and special situations . . . We remain really disciplined on valuation. Valuation really hasn't mattered over the last five or six years. So it's kind of just rocketed up from bottom left to top right of the page and resulted in expensive valuations. But it will eventually; valuation does matter. And so we've been very, very disciplined there and continue to be. And we remain diversified from an underlying

economic exposure and a market returns perspective, so we are mindful of
the share price correlations, but we also look at the underlying economic
exposures of our business.'

Jessica Amir is a market analyst at Bell Direct.

'One: each pay I invest into the market and I also reassess my investments.
So that's a part of my investment philosophy. Two: I look at buying shares
like how I would look at buying a business, much like what Warren Buffett
recommends . . . It's important to back good management . . . good management is key—find companies with [a] track record of success. Think about
buying shares like you're buying a business, with strong management and
growing earnings.'

One investor's framework in detail

Owen Raszkiewicz is the founder of Rask Australia, an investment
news, education and research network.

We spoke to Owen about his investment process and he gave us
ten rules that underpin his investing strategy. We thought they were a
great summary of an investing framework, so here they are.

1 Capitalism works. If companies and entrepreneurs create value for
   society by solving problems, shareholders supporting them must be
   rewarded.
2 The stock market is a vehicle for transferring wealth from the
   impatient to the patient.
3 Wealth creation can be summed up in two words: accumulate assets.
4 Fewer investment decisions often result in better decisions, so high
   conviction and concentration is the best approach when you know
   what you are doing.
5 Diversification is very important for beginners, passive and index
   investors—including the tens of millions of people who have better
   things to do than manage an investment portfolio.

6 That said, for professionals, the benefits of extra diversification rapidly diminish after ten unique positions.

7 Less than 5% of companies on the stock market are responsible for all of the market's excess returns.

8 There are three commonly accepted investing 'edges': behaviour, analytical ability and information. Investors would be wise to focus first and foremost on their behaviour.

9 Most people shouldn't invest in individual shares because they lack the time, inclination and/or curiosity, each of which is required to invest well over time.

10 Investors do not need to choose between 'active' or 'passive'— everyone should consider using both.

Understanding diversification

One of the most common terms you'll hear in investing is 'diversification'. It's a term that's thrown around a lot, but often misunderstood. At its core, diversification is a critical way to lower the risk of losing all your money. In this section we cover everything you need to know and, more importantly, how to practically apply it to your investing.

Never put all your eggs in one basket.

It's an important lesson for all investors. There are a lot of risks that come with investing—a company could go bankrupt, a new technology could disrupt an industry, a country could go into recession.

If all your eggs are in one basket (aka all your money in one stock), one event could crack all those eggs. An important thing to always remember is to spread your eggs across multiple baskets.

This process of spreading your investments, so they are not all exposed to one source of risk, is called **diversification**.

PARDON THE JARGON
diversification

Diversification refers to spreading your money across a number of different investments. By owning a wide variety of different assets in a portfolio, you reduce the risk of losing all the money you invested. If one investment loses value, the other investments are still there to protect your overall wealth.

At the end of the day, diversification is all about avoiding losing all your money. We've had some firsthand experiences with what a lack of diversification can do when things go wrong.

The risk of not diversifying—my first investment

 ALEC
When I started my investing journey, I thought all I could invest in was individual stocks. I saved and saved, and when I was ready I looked in the paper for a stock to invest in. I found a law firm that had grown a lot and was getting a lot of positive reporting in the media—Slater & Gordon Lawyers.

I took the money I had saved and invested it all in this one company. Within one year I had lost 95% of my money. Within two years I had lost 99%.

Slater & Gordon had been improperly accounting for the amount of money they were making and the UK government changed a law that disastrously impacted their UK business. Their share price collapsed, and with it the value of my investment.

This was my only investment. So with Slater & Gordon's collapse, I lost all of the money I saved.

If I had invested in two companies rather than just the one, this Slater & Gordon would've only seen me lose half of my money rather than all of it. That, in a nutshell, is the importance of diversification.

How much is too much?

Once you understand the importance of diversification, the question becomes: how much to diversify?

If Alec had owned shares in two companies rather than just Slater & Gordon, he would have lost only half his money. If he had owned shares in four companies, when Slater & Gordon collapsed he would have lost only a quarter of his money.

How far do you extend that? If he had owned 100 stocks, then Slater & Gordon would have been only 1% of his whole portfolio. Or if he owned 1,000 stocks then Slater & Gordon would have been only 0.1%.

This leads to one of the most common questions asked in the Equity Mates community.

 LISTENER QUESTION

how many stocks do I need to be diversified?

This is a tricky question; there's no straight answer. We can't say you need to own at least five stocks. Or at least ten stocks. Everyone's risk tolerance is different, so this answer is unique to you.

There are some key rules of thumb that can help you answer this question for yourself.

The first thing to understand is that the more stocks you own, the less you stand to lose if one stock falls. If we look at professional fund managers, a standard investment fund will hold between 25 and 40 stocks. Funds that hold between 10 and 15 stocks are known as 'more concentrated' and are generally considered higher risk.

The second thing to note is that there are diminishing returns the more you diversify. Academic studies show that once you go beyond 20–25 stocks, there isn't that much less risk. Portfolios with more than 25 stocks show the same risk levels of those with 25 stocks. The reason for this is, once you hit 25 stocks, you generally have a pretty good spread across different industries (e.g. some retail, some banks, some mining etc.) and different countries (e.g. some make their money in Australia, others in the USA, others in Asia).

The different kinds of risk

If the point of diversification is to reduce risk, a question that follows is: what do we mean by risk?

Simply, it is the risk of losing money—the risk of your investments being worth less than when you bought them. At the end of the day, the reason you invest (and probably the reason you bought *Get Started Investing*) is to make money.

'Risk of losing money' is pretty broad. There are plenty of reasons an investment could go down and an investor could lose money. When we're thinking about diversification of our investments, we like to think about the different categories of risk.

- Individual company risk: these are risks specific to each individual company. These include things like poor management, bad business strategy and other risks that things go wrong at the company.
- Industry risk: there are risks that a whole industry might suffer or be disrupted by new technology or business models. For example, Amazon introducing online shopping has disrupted the whole bricks-and-mortar retail industry. Or government regulations on carbon emissions have hurt the oil and gas industry.
- Asset-class risk: These are risks that might affect a whole asset class (e.g. property or shares). For example, if the Australian government changed the tax policy on negative gearing, house prices would suffer, affecting property as an asset class. Similarly, if NASA succeed in mining gold on an asteroid (yes, that is something it is looking at doing), the increase in the supply of gold would hurt gold as an asset class.
- Country risk: if something goes wrong in a particular country, then many of the investments in that country will go down. For example, if Australia goes into recession then Australians will be looking to tighten their belts and won't have as much to spend on investing, hurting all different asset classes in Australia. Given your job is most likely based in Australia, you are heavily reliant on the Australian economy. Diversify this risk by owning overseas investments.

Given these different categories of risk, we think the most important thing when thinking about diversification is to ensure you're not overly exposed to any one source of risk.

For example, if you own twenty Australian stocks and a house in Australia, then if something happens to the Australian economy all of your investments will suffer.

Alternatively, if you owned shares in Coles, Woolworths, Walmart and Costco, a recession in Australia would only hurt the Australian supermarkets (Coles and Woolworths) but would not hurt the American supermarkets (Walmart and Costco). But all four of these companies are grocery retailers, so a big change in the way we buy food (ordering all our meals from UberEATS or getting our groceries from Hello Fresh) would affect all four of these companies.

Tying it all together: how to think about diversification

As you can see, diversification is a big topic. At a high level it is easy to understand—don't put all your eggs in one basket—but when you're looking at your own investments, it is a lot harder to figure out if you're diversified enough.

Here are a few simple points that we use in our personal investing to help us think about diversification.

- Don't own just one type of investment. Have some stocks, some cash savings, some property (and don't worry, you can own property without signing up to a 30-year mortgage—we're about to get into that).
- Get outside your home country. With technology, it has never been easier to access overseas markets. Make sure you have some investments outside Australia, so if things go wrong in Australia your whole portfolio doesn't suffer.
- Own stocks across different industries. No matter how much you love a particular industry, spread your investments around to reduce your risk.

- Buy diversified products. You can buy products that track indexes (those groups of stocks we introduced earlier). These are naturally diversified because there are so many different companies in an index. You can also invest in managed investment funds that hold multiple investments. These products have in-built diversity and are an easy way to build diversification into your portfolio (don't worry, we'll explain this more later).
- Don't worry about diversifying all at once. None of this means you need to invest in ten-plus stocks from Day 1. Build diversification in your portfolio over time.

What can I invest in?

We're about to take you to school. Welcome to asset class.

There are plenty of different choices for you to invest in. These different choices are called **asset classes**.

 PARDON THE JARGON
assets and asset classes

An **asset** is any resource that can be owned or controlled and has economic value. Everything from your house or your car to a business's intellectual property is an asset.

An **asset class** is a group of assets grouped by their financial characteristics. Examples include 'property', which captures everything from residential housing to office buildings to farmland, or 'cash and currency', which includes all national currencies (such as the Australian dollar, Japanese yen etc.) and cryptocurrency (such as Bitcoin).

Almost every asset class can be invested in through the stock market. Yes, the name is a little misleading. You can buy far more than just stocks on the stock market. Here are a few of the major options available.

What are your options through the stock market?

Individual companies

This is the most common form of investment on the stock market. You buy a share and become a part-owner of the company.

Professional investors

If you don't want to make decisions yourself, you can invest in the company of a professional investor. The investor uses this company to invest in shares, and when the professional investor makes money from investing in the right companies, you make money.

A whole industry or the whole market

There are plenty of funds that give you a little bit of everything. You can invest in index funds that track market indexes we introduced earlier. There are similar funds that track a particular industry (for example, the Australian technology industry or the global banking industry).

Property

House prices out of reach? Fear not, the stock market allows you to buy 'Real Estate Investment Trusts'—basically companies that own property. If the property market goes up, you benefit, without having to sign up to a 30-year mortgage.

Government and company debt (also known as bonds)

Governments and companies often need to borrow money to fund their operations. You can buy this debt through the stock market and have the government or companies pay you back, with interest.

Commodities

Gold, oil, coal, wheat. All of these are commodities that are traded in the market. You can invest in these commodities (as well as plenty more) and make money if their price goes up.

Cash and currencies

There are 180 currencies around the world. Every day they change in value against each other and investors make money investing in currencies they think will get more valuable.

Don't forget about your super

When you are thinking about investing options, don't forget about your superannuation. For those non-Australians, this is a retirement savings account that every Australian in a paying job is required to have. (It would be similar to a compulsory 401k in America.)

This forced retirement saving is invested across a variety of asset classes. Most accounts will have a combination of stocks, bonds, property, currency and infrastructure among a variety of investments.

Many people don't think about super as an investment. Which means these people are investing without even knowing it (not bad . . .).

It is worth thinking about super as an investment and consciously factoring it into your thinking. It can become a critical part of your investing strategy.

 LISTENER QUESTION
should I contribute more to super or invest outside super?

When you start thinking about your super as an investment, this is a really good question to ask. You have the choice of asking your employer to put more of your salary into your super account rather than paying you in salary. It becomes a dilemma: should I ask my employer to allocate it to super (and invest that way) or get paid and then invest it personally outside super?

One of the big factors in this decision used to be the control over your investment options. If you allocated it to super, your super fund would invest it without you having any control, which was great for people who didn't want to think about it, but didn't work for people who wanted to invest it in a particular asset class. But these days, new platforms are giving Australians more control over how their super is invested, so this is less of a factor.

For us, there are two big factors to consider. How you balance these factors is a personal decision and will give you an indication of how you should answer this question.

1. Tax—the biggest reason to contribute more to super. Any money contributed to your super account is taxed at 15%. Compare this to the 32.5% tax rate for the average Australian salary, and there is a serious tax advantage to invest this money through super rather than outside super.
2. Time—the biggest reason to invest outside super. If you invest through your super account you cannot access this money until you're 65. Think about your investing goals and when you will need to access this money. If you're investing to be comfortable in retirement, then great. If you're investing to be able to afford private school fees for your kids, then this timing may not work.

For us, balancing the money saved from the lower tax rate with the fact that the money is then locked up until we turn 65 is the key decision when deciding how to invest with super and how much to invest outside super.

How to get the most out of your super

One of the best things about super is that it is automatic. You don't have to think about it, you can't touch it and it just compounds and compounds for decades. Ideally growing into a meaningful nest egg for your retirement.

There are a few things you should do to ensure you're set up optimally.

The steps in the checklist below are worth working through. It's worth thinking about how your super is set up; don't just leave it on autopilot for the early part of your working life. If your super is set up correctly in your twenties and thirties, you're giving yourself a much better chance to retire with a larger amount of money in your sixties or seventies.

- Don't just use your employer's default super account. It may not be the right one for you, and you could be losing out on better returns. Check your options, do some research online and speak to a financial adviser if you have one. It is really easy to change super accounts if your default account isn't the best.
- Check the fees you're paying and compare them to other funds. Fees can have a big impact on your overall returns, so make sure you're minimising your fees.
- Ensure you're happy with your insurance and other arrangements. Many people don't know, but their superannuation account comes with a life insurance policy as a default option. Which you pay for out of your super. If you're young, single and don't have any dependants, think about whether you really need life insurance. If you decide you don't need it, make sure you aren't paying for it.

- Make sure you're happy with the investment strategy. Many super funds allow you to choose between 'conservative', 'balanced' or 'aggressive' settings. As a general rule of thumb you want to be aggressive while you're younger (because your account can really start compounding early and has decades to recover any losses) and then get more conservative as you get older (because not losing money becomes more important the closer you are to retirement).

How do I make money?

So we've just spent a thousand words telling you what you can invest in. While there are plenty of options for you to invest in, the good news is, there are only two ways that you make money when investing. We'll cover them off in this section.

There are two ways you make money when investing, either by selling an investment for a higher price than you paid or buying something that then pays you income. The good news? For a lot of investments you don't have to choose and you can make money both ways.

The first way to make money: you sell it for more than you bought it

Every day, the price of shares moves on the stock market. You can check them at any time and see what price you can sell them at. If the shares you own have gone up, and you sell, you make the difference between the price you bought and the price you sold. If you buy 1 share for $100, and then sell it for $120, you've made $20. It really is that simple.

That's the same for a number of other assets. If you buy a house the difference between the price you buy at and the price you sell at is the money you make.

The change in the price of an asset is known as a **capital gain** (if it goes up) or a **capital loss** (if it goes down).

PARDON THE JARGON
capital gain and capital loss

Capital gain is the term used for the money made on the sale of an asset. Money made by selling a house, a share, a car, a business, any other asset is known as a capital gain.

Alternatively, if you lose money after selling an asset (i.e. if you sell a car for less than you paid) then that is known as a **capital loss**.

The second way to make money: buy something that pays you

You can make money by selling an investment for more than you paid. You can also make money while you hold an investment.

Similar to the way your bank pays you interest on savings in the bank, many investments, including stocks, pay you while you are holding an investment. This introduces a common investing term, **dividend**.

PARDON THE JARGON
dividend

A **dividend** is a payment from a company to its shareholders.

When a company makes a profit, it has a few choices of what to do with that money. The two main options are to keep that profit and reinvest it into the business (hire more staff, develop new products, expand into new countries etc.) or the second option is to give that money to the owners of the business. Usually a company will do a bit of both: keep some profit to reinvest in the business and pay some of the profit out to shareholders.

When a company pays profit to shareholders, it is called a dividend. The company will pay a set amount for each share and an investor gets paid for the number of shares they hold.

For example, if a company announces it will pay a dividend of $1 per share and you own 100 shares, the company will pay you $100.

In Australia, dividends are usually paid twice per year.

It is important to note that not every company pays a dividend. It is up to the individual company whether it pays a dividend or not. The majority of established Australian companies do choose to pay a dividend.

Similarly, investments like bonds (the term for the debt of governments and companies) pay investors while they hold these investments. The term for these bond payments is 'yield'.

LISTENER QUESTION

is there a difference between dividends, interest and yield?

In a nutshell, no. These are all different terms for cash payments to investors.

- For savings accounts, these cash payments are called interest.
- For bonds, these cash payments are called bond yield.
- For stocks, these cash payments are called dividends.

While they are different terms, they all mean the same thing: money in your account.

With stocks, you don't have to choose

For a lot of assets, you can only make money one way or the other. If you buy a bar of gold or the house that you live in, you don't earn any income and you rely on making a capital gain (i.e. selling it for more than you bought it for). On the other hand, any money you save in a term deposit or high-interest saving account will earn income (in the form of interest) but you cannot make a capital gain.

There are a few assets where you are able to earn both income and a capital gain. Buying a property to rent is one major way, and stocks are the other.

We've got a few examples that illustrate how you can make money both through capital gains and dividends by owning stocks.

If you'd bought $1,000 of Woolworths stock 5 years ago

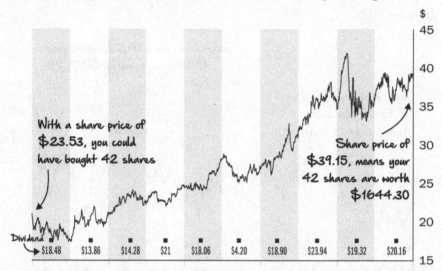

With a share price of $23.53, you could have bought 42 shares

Share price of $39.15, means your 42 shares are worth $1644.30

Dividend

$18.48 $13.86 $14.28 $21 $18.06 $4.20 $18.90 $23.94 $19.32 $20.16

By buying 42 shares of Woolworths, you would have turned $988.26 into $1816.50 in 5 years. This $828.24 you made would have come from $656.04 in capital gains and $172.20 in dividends.

If you'd bought $1,000 of Wesfarmers stock 5 years ago

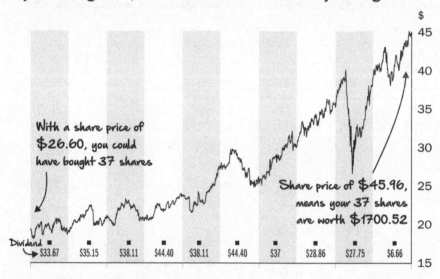

With a share price of $26.60, you could have bought 37 shares

Share price of $45.96, means your 37 shares are worth $1700.52

Dividend

$33.67 $35.15 $38.11 $44.40 $38.11 $44.40 $37 $28.86 $27.75 $6.66

By buying 37 shares of Wesfarmers, you would have turned $984.20 into $2034.63 in 5 years. This $1050.43 you made would have come from $716.32 in capital gains and $334.11 in dividends.

If you'd bought $1,000 of Commonwealth Bank stock 5 years ago

Share price of $69.02, means your 13 shares are worth $897.26

With a share price of $75.76, you could have bought 13 shares

Dividend $25.74 $28.86 $25.87 $29.90 $26 $30.03 $26 $30.03 $26 $12.74

2016   2017   2018   2019   2020   2021

By buying 13 shares of Commonwealth Bank, you would've turned $984.88 into $1158.43 in 5 years. This is despite the share price actually going down. You would have actually lost $87.62 by the share price falling from $75.76 to $69.02. But, over the 5 years, you would have been paid $261.17 in dividends.

Fees

Fools pay fees. The #1 thing you can do to maximise your investment returns is to minimise any unnecessary fees.

The effect that fees can have on an investment portfolio over a few decades is pretty hard to comprehend.

At the start of *Get Started Investing*, we introduced the concept of compounding and how consistent returns over a long period of time can start growing into a pretty incredible amount of money. If fees reduce this consistent return year after year, they can have a massive impact over time.

Sometimes fees are labelled as 'expense ratio' or 'management costs' but, whatever they're called, they mean the same thing. Less money for you at the end of the day.

Fees are usually charged as a percentage of the amount invested. For example, if you put your money in a fund that charges 1% in fees, that means every year 1% of your money is taken as fees. Let's say this fund makes 10% every year. This is how the fees would work:

- You start by putting $100 into the fund.
- At the end of Year 1, the fund makes 10% so add $10 to your $100, giving you $110.
- The fund then takes its 1% fee ($1.10 off $110), leaving you with $108.90 after fees.
- At the end of Year 2, the fund has made another 10% so add $10.89 to your $108.90, giving you $119.79.

- Once again, the fund then takes 1% ($1.19 off $119.79), leaving you with $118.60.

To show the effect even a small difference in fees can have over a long period of time, look at the comparison below.

	10% a year with no fees	10% a year with 1% fee	10% a year with 2% fee
Starting amount	$1,000	$1,000	$1,000
Year 1	$1,100	$1,089	$1,078
Year 2	$1,210	$1,186	$1,162
Year 3	$1,331	$1,291	$1,253
Year 4	$1,464	$1,406	$1,350
Year 5	$1,611	$1,532	$1,456
Year 10	$2,594	$2,346	$2,119
Year 20	$6,727	$5,502	$4,491
Year 30	$17,449	$12,907	$9,518
Year 40	$45,259	$30,277	$20,172

That difference in Year 40 is a big reason why minimising the fees is so important. Over the long term, it can make a massive difference.

Basically, whatever you pay in fees you need to make up in additional investing returns. If you're going to get the similar returns from two different choices—the better choice is the one with lower fees.

WARREN BUFFETT
the effect of fees

Warren Buffett is the greatest investor of all time, and, like every investor, we have the chance to invest in his company, Berkshire Hathaway.

When Buffett took over Berkshire Hathaway in 1965 it was a failing textile manufacturer. In the 55 years since, Buffett has produced an incredible investing track record and made all of his investors a lot of money.

In this time, he has achieved over 2 million per cent return.

In practical terms, if you had invested $1,000 with Buffett in 1965, you would now have over $27 million! But if Buffett had charged fees on this money you wouldn't have $27 million.

- If he charged a 1% fee, you would have $25 million.
- If he charged a 2% fee, you would have $9 million.
- If he charged 2% and then a 20% performance fee (traditional investment fund fees), you would have $6.5 million.

Small differences in fees can make a big difference.

Know what you're paying

Here's what you can do to minimise what you're paying. The first step is to know *what* you're paying.

There are three major categories of fees you need to be aware of:

1 When buying or selling—there are often costs associated with buying or selling any investment (this is known as 'brokerage'). You need to be aware of how much you're paying and if there are cheaper ways to buy or sell the same thing. This may also include overseas transaction fees if you're buying something overseas.

2 When others are managing your money—if you are putting your money into a managed investment fund, an index fund or anything similar where a company manages your money there will likely be a management fee attached. This includes your super fund.

3 To access different products and services—there are some great resources out there to give you access to the stock market or information about it. Just be mindful of how much you are paying for this access or information.

Of these three categories, the most important is the second. These management fees, year after year, can really start to add up. You should always be checking the fees on an investment product and if there is a similar product with lower fees.

How to find out what you're paying

Okay, so fees are important. Where do you find them?

Any fund or exchange-traded fund (ETF) you're investing in will disclose their fees. There are two key places to look for this information. The first is the Product Disclosure Statement (often shortened to PDS) that lists all key details about the investing product.

The second place to look is on the fund's website. Every fund will state the fees it charges on its website. Confusingly, there are a variety of terms used for 'fees'. Some of the most commonly used are expense ratio, management fee or management expense ratio. Watch out for these terms, and remember: at the end of the day, they all mean the same thing.

Always check your fees

As an example of the difference fees can make, here we have two funds that track the S&P 500 index (America's major stock market index). You can see on the final line that they have different expense ratios. One charges 0.04% and the other, 0.09%.

	IVV	SPY
Name	iShares Core S&P 500 ETF	SPDR S&P 500 ETF
Category	Large Cap Blend Equities	Large Cap Blend Equities
Index	S&P 500 Index	S&P 500 Index
Expense Ratio	0.04%	0.09%

While they may not seem like major differences, these little differences do add up over time. Also, why would you pay any more than you need to?

As part of your research, you can check what each fund holds. As you can see from the side-by-side comparison below, each fund holds the same companies. If they both hold the same companies, why would you pay more fees?

IVV All 506 Holdings		SPY All 506 Holdings	
Holding	Weighting	Holding	Weighting
Apple Inc (AAPL)	3.94%	Apple Inc (AAPL)	3.96%
Microsoft Corp (MSFT)	2.63%	Microsoft Corp (MSFT)	2.63%
Facebook Inc (FB)	1.9%	Facebook Inc (FB)	1.91%
Amazon.com Inc (AMZN)	1.83%	Amazon.com Inc (AMZN)	1.83%
Johnson & Johnson (JNJ)	1.68%	Johnson & Johnson (JNJ)	1.69%
EXXon Mobil Corp (XOM)	1.60%	EXXon Mobil Corp (XOM)	1.60%
Berkshire Hathaway Inc (BRK.B)	1.59%	Berkshire Hathaway Inc (BRK.B)	1.59%
JPMorgan Chase & Co (JPM)	1.56%	JPMorgan Chase & Co (JPM)	1.57%
Alphabet Inc (GOOGL)	1.31%	Alphabet Inc (GOOGL)	1.32%
Alphabet Inc (GOOG)	1.29%	Alphabet Inc (GOOG)	1.30%
Bank of America Corp (BAC)	1.16%	Bank of America Corp (BAC)	1.16%
Wells Fargo & Co (WFC)	1.11%	Wells Fargo & Co (WFC)	1.12%
AT&T Inc (T)	1.11%	AT&T Inc (T)	1.11%
Proctor & Gamble Co (PG)	1.10%	Proctor & Gamble Co (PG)	1.11%

Comparing fees is especially important when it comes to your super-annuation account. All super funds charge fees. The difference in these fees can be quite a lot. Go on your super fund's website, check what it charges and then start googling. See what other funds are out there and what fees they charge.

When are fees worth it?

One important caveat to this discussion is—sometimes fees can be worth it.

We know that's a little confusing, but stick with us.

We aren't saying you should completely avoid fees. We are all about minimising them when they're not necessary.

So, when would we be happy to pay fees?

There are two scenarios when we'd be happy to pay fees: when an investment option is better or when it is unique. Outside these two broad reasons, we'd be reluctant to pay more fees than we absolutely had to.

1 Better

There are some incredibly smart and capable investors out there. The opportunity to give our money to them and have them invest it on our behalf is pretty incredible. A lot of them charge higher fees but invest far better than your average professional manager could (or we could ourselves). For these investors, we would be happy to pay higher than average fees.

The most important thing to watch in these situations is your return *after fees*. It doesn't help you if your fund manager is getting 15% returns every year, if—after they charge their fees—you are only getting market average returns. If you're going to pay higher fees, you better be getting higher returns *after fees*.

The majority of professional investors don't outperform the market year after year, after fees. When we say 'better' we really do mean 'better'. It's your hard-earned money; you should only entrust it with the best of the best.

2 Unique

The second situation where we would be happy to pay higher fees is for unique situations. The example we gave above about an S&P 500 index fund is not unique. There are plenty of funds that offer access to the S&P 500 index. They are all much the same. There is no reason to pay higher fees for the same thing.

The opposite situation is where you have the opportunity to invest in something that is truly unique. If you want to invest in a fund that invests in Australian water rights or Brazilian technology start-ups, you will need to pay higher than usual fees. There's nothing wrong with this, as long as you've done your research and have come to the conclusion that this is the right investment for you.

Tips to reduce your fees

Here are some of the tips we've picked up from our personal investing journeys and speaking to experts.

- Track your expenses. Always know what you're paying in fees.
- Do your research, and check what's out there. Can you get the same thing with lower fees?
- Be mindful of how much you're investing. Don't put all your investments in high fee funds.

Section summary
YOUR PROGRESS

☑ WHY INVEST
☑ BUILD AN INVESTOR MINDSET
☑ GET YOUR MONEY RIGHT

☑ UNDERSTANDING THE BASICS

There's a lot to understand when it comes to the world of investing, and with all the new concepts, jargon and charts it can get confusing. In this section we covered all the basics you need to know. You may not feel like you know everything, and that's okay. Over time you'll build your knowledge and build your confidence. But at this point, you know enough to get started.

You have:
✓ learnt some key concepts: shares, markets and indexes
✓ understood the different styles of investing
✓ recognised the importance of diversification
✓ seen some of the different options you have to invest in and understood how you make money investing.

☐ TAKING THE PLUNGE
☐ BEYOND THE FIRST INVESTMENT
☐ LESSONS WE WISH WE HAD KNOWN
☐ PULLING IT ALL TOGETHER

PART 6

Taking the Plunge

By now we hope we've convinced you that investing in stocks is the right thing to do. You understand some of the basics and realise that it's nowhere near as hard as you first thought.

Now it's time to make your first investment!

Start small (micro-investing)

Now that we've answered 'why invest?' and helped you understand some of the basics, the next question is 'how do you start?'

The great news is that it has never been easier to get started investing.

Technology has reduced the costs and complexity involved in this process. These days you can get started simply by signing up to an app.

You've probably heard that finding a broker is the first step to start investing. Well, that's not entirely true, thanks to micro-investing. We touched on micro-investing earlier in Part 4, but there are a few more details we want to cover. It's such a great way for you to enter the market as your first step.

What is micro-investing?

Micro-investing, otherwise known as loose-change investing, is a way to invest your spare change.

So throw out your piggy bank. With technology you can put this loose change in the stock market instead.

Sounds easy, right? It is!

Micro-investing takes your dollars and cents from everyday transactions and combines them with the money from other investors like you. It then uses this money to invest in the stock market.

It's all in the name: 'micro'. The idea is you regularly invest very small amounts of money, sometimes literally cents, eventually building up to a portfolio that is more significant in value.

For people who don't have a lot of money to invest, and don't know a lot about investing, it is a great way to get some exposure to the stock market.

Is micro-investing for me?

It is daunting taking the first step.

Thankfully, micro-investing is here to help.

If it's not clear by now, you can start with dollars and cents.

When we started our investing journeys, back in the early 2000s, the minimum needed was $500. Saving that amount was challenging, a huge barrier. Then, to make a second investment, we needed to save another minimum $500.

This minimum still does apply to many brokers in the Australian market (at the time of writing) but thanks to micro-investing apps, it's not the only avenue you have to take. Forget the idea you need to save large sums of money to kickstart your journey.

You *do* have enough money to get started.

Micro-investing is set up so that you don't have to do a lot of thinking. You don't need to know a lot about the markets to start.

When micro-investing companies take your loose change from everyday transactions, or from small voluntary contributions, they are pooling these funds with all the other investors doing the same thing.

They take that pool of money and put it into share-based investments.

POOL YOUR MONEY

You don't have to choose what specific companies to buy.

You don't have to choose what exchange-traded funds (ETFs) to buy (although you can if you want to).

You don't have to know how much to allocate to bonds or cash or gold.

If you don't understand any of those terms, that's fine, because you don't have to.

Micro-investing apps are designed for you to get enough exposure to the markets without it feeling daunting. Purely by being active on the apps, you will slowly come to understand some of those terms. That's what's great about it.

So, you *do* have enough money to start and you *do* have enough knowledge.

Take the emotion out of investing

Knowing when to buy and when to sell is one of the most common questions we get. And there is no clear-cut answer. There are many variables you need to consider, some of which we will unpack in a later section.

Often, people who are new to investing will make these decisions based on emotion. It's easy to get carried away and influenced by the media, friends and family, who may be saying 'now's the time to buy'. Equally, when the market is tanking, and you're watching some of your hard-earned dollars shrinking, it's hard to not feel like you should be selling.

One of the major advantages of setting up recurring deposits through micro-investing apps is a strategy known as **dollar-cost averaging**, or DCA.

PARDON THE JARGON
dollar-cost averaging (DCA)

Dollar-cost averaging is where you invest smaller, fixed amounts on a regular basis. It's generally done over an extended period.

For example, you may have $2,000 you want to invest. Rather than investing the lot at once, you might invest $20 every fortnight.

The beauty of recurring deposits—regular, fixed amounts—is that it takes away the emotion of buying and selling. Regardless of what the market is doing, whether it's up or whether it's down, you will invest the same amount each time. You don't have to think about it. The micro-investing app will withdraw your designated amount, and invest it. Done!

What this means is that when the market is down you will buy more and when the market is up you will buy less. Rather than risking all of your money at once, you buy into the market often, reducing the effect of the market moving up and down.

What am I investing in?

Each micro-investing app is different but, in general, these apps offer you a number of options to get broad exposure to the market.

What do we mean by broad exposure?

If you were to invest all of your money into one stock, like Afterpay, you would have very limited exposure to the market. All of your returns, or losses, will be solely due to the performance of Afterpay's stock price. This is like putting all of your eggs in one basket.

Having limited exposure can be good, if the stock does really well. Equally, if it doesn't do so well, then you don't have anything else in your portfolio to balance out the loss. In other words, if you drop your basket, then all your eggs will smash, leaving you with no eggs.

Broad exposure, on the other hand, is where you have many investments across a range of different sectors of the market, and different asset classes (which we spoke about in Part 5). Having many investments, or eggs in many baskets, reduces your risk of losing money.

Why?

Let's use the eggs in baskets as an example. If you put your eggs in many baskets, and drop one basket, only the eggs in that basket will smash, with the others remaining intact. Same goes for stocks. If your money is in many investments, and one doesn't perform, you have the other investments to balance it out.

Micro-investing apps try to put your eggs in many baskets. For example, a portfolio of investments might consist of:

- cash (the Australian dollar)
- large Australian companies, like BHP, Commonwealth Bank and Telstra
- large Asian companies, like Samsung, Hyundai and Tencent
- large European companies, like Nestlé, Volkswagen and Unilever
- large US companies, like Apple, Microsoft and Google
- government **bonds**.

When you invest your round-ups, lump sums or recurring deposits, you will get a little bit of everything in that portfolio, spreading your eggs, or money, across many baskets, or investments.

SPREAD YOUR MONEY

Australian stocks

International stocks

Property

Cash

!&?# PARDON THE JARGON
bonds

Bonds are just the investing term for debt. When companies and governments need to borrow money they don't have to go to a bank. Instead they can go to investors and borrow money from them.

When a company or government borrows money from an investor, it creates a 'bond'. It is a contract that says how much money it is borrowing, when it has to pay the money back and any interest it has to pay.

The investor can hold that bond and collect the interest and wait to get paid back. Or they can sell that bond to other investors.

If you think about the Australian government, every year it presents the Budget, and the media discuss how we are in a budget deficit. Basically, we are spending more money than we are bringing in from taxes. The government is able to get this extra money by selling bonds to investors.

How does it actually work?

Micro-investing takes whatever you want to invest, combines it with all other investors' money, and together invests it on behalf of the group. You can't buy individual stocks like Commonwealth Bank or Microsoft. Instead, you own a fraction of what the app invests in on behalf of the group.

There are three main ways that you can manage and interact with micro-investing apps.

1 Round-ups

This is the first place to start and one of the most common features of micro-investing apps. It works by you linking your debit cards to the app. Then, for every transaction you make, it will round up to the nearest dollar and invest the difference.

For example, if you were to buy a drink for $4.50, it will round up to $5 and invest the $0.50. It's that easy. Some apps will accumulate the spare change, until it reaches a minimum amount of say $5, and will then invest that $5.

If you think about how many transactions you make on your card these days, it's easy to see that over time you can start to build a decent-sized portfolio, without needing to make any significant change to your spending or saving behaviour.

2 Lump sums

Once you're comfortable with your spare change coming out of your account, and you have a bit of a handle on the apps, you can think about additional contributions. Let's say you get to the end of the month and you have a spare $50 that you didn't spend.

A great way to invest this, without needing to make too many decisions, is to make a lump sum deposit into your micro-investing app.

By transferring into the app, it will take your lump sum and invest it into the same share-based investments that your spare change is going into. It's very simple, and a great way to get added exposure to the stock market. You can continue to do this as often as you like, building up your portfolio faster than if you were to rely on just the round-ups.

3 Recurring deposits

If you like the idea of the round-ups, but want to grow your portfolio faster, then setting up a recurring deposit is a great option. In addition to your round-ups, you can automatically add extra money at a regular frequency.

You might choose to add an extra $5 per week, or $20 a fortnight. Whatever it may be, the apps easily allow you to set this up. It will then automatically withdraw the money from your account at each interval, and invest it into the portfolio you have chosen.

Again, this is a great way to boost your portfolio and get exposure to the stock market, without needing a lot of cash upfront or a lot of knowledge about investing.

Can I withdraw my money?

Short answer: yes.

You can sell your investments whenever you like, and withdraw the money. Given you are selling investments, you generally don't get your money immediately. Each micro-investing app has a processing time between selling and when you receive the money back in your account.

The key thing to know is that you're not locked in. You can withdraw your money if you need to. But the longer you keep it in there, the more opportunity you are giving compounding to do its work.

Is it expensive?

Each micro-investing app is different and charges different fees, but here are some that you should be aware of:

- Brokerage—you may be charged a flat fee, or a percentage, each time you make an investment. We'll cover this in more detail when we discuss brokers.
- Account fees—some of the apps charge a monthly account fee if your balance exceeds a certain amount: for example, $5,000. This fee is generally a percentage of the balance amount.
- Maintenance fees—while the apps are free to set up, some charge a flat monthly maintenance fee.

Not all the apps charge the same fees, so it's important you have a look at your specific provider to understand what it is charging.

Always be mindful of fees

  ALEC & BRYCE

At Equity Mates, we hate fees (it's one of our three official policies). When you use a micro-investing app, always be mindful of the fees you're paying.

A lot of the time, the fees may look small (e.g. $1 per year). But if you're only investing a small amount, those fees can add up.

Let's say you invest $5 per year. If you pay $1 in fees, that's 20% of your total amount. This means your remaining $4 needs to go up 25% (25% of $4 is $1) just to get back to your original $5.

When looking at fees, look at it as a percentage of your investment. Our rule of thumb is: always pay less than 1% in fees. If you have to pay $1 per year, you'd want at least $100 invested.

Pros and cons of micro-investing

As with everything in life, micro-investing has pros and cons. Here are the major points for you to weigh up.

Pros

- No deposit is needed to start.
- No investing knowledge required to get going.
- Very convenient.
- Provides diversification and broad market exposure.
- Can set and forget—removes emotion from buying and selling.

Cons

- You may get better returns elsewhere if you know what you're doing.
- Limited options in what you can invest in.
- Fees can be high, depending how you use the apps.

Key providers in Australia

There are three big micro-investing platforms in Australia that you can research. This list is current as of our time of writing but make sure you do your own research—a simple google search of 'micro-investing apps Australia' will show you your options.

We are not recommending any particular platform, just providing you information on what is out there, so we have presented the below in alphabetical order.

- CommSec Pocket offers investors the ability to invest from as little as $50. Transfer money into the app and you can buy into funds that follow different markets (e.g. Australia, America) or different themes (e.g. tech, sustainability).
- Raiz rounds up your transactions and invests that spare change in the stock market. Bought a $4.50 coffee? Raiz rounds that purchase up to $5, takes the $0.50 and invests it for you.
- Spaceship Voyager has no minimum investment amount and no fees until your account is over $5,000. It offers investors two choices: tracking the market or a fund managed by professional investors.

The process of buying and selling stocks

It's all well and good understanding the basics, but it's important to understand what goes on under the hood. The process of buying and selling stocks is an important piece of information to know.

When you think of buying and selling stocks, think of how a movie star finds their next movie. Most of the time they don't do the work; they have an agent who does it on their behalf.

It's the same process in the stock market. You don't need to find someone to sell you a stock. Instead, you get an agent (known as a broker) to do it on your behalf.

In its most basic form, here's how the buying and selling process works on the stock market.

A buyer puts an order in to buy a stock	A seller puts an order in to sell a stock
An agent takes that order and looks for a seller	An agent takes that order and looks for a buyer
Agent matches with a seller and agrees a price	Agent matches with a buyer and agrees a price
Agent pays the seller and takes the stock in return	Agent gives the stock to the buyer and takes the buyer's money
The stock is placed in the buyer's account	The money is placed in the seller's account

The best way to think about this process is like buying a house. There's someone who wants to sell, and someone who wants to buy, and the real estate agent is in the middle finding two parties who will agree on a price. In the stock market, that agent is known as a broker.

Let's take a closer look at what you need to know about brokers.

How do I actually buy? Brokers

Before anyone can buy a share, they must have a broker. Some of the most common questions we're asked are 'How do I buy stocks?' and 'What broker should I use?'

By now you understand why investing is important, and the huge opportunity it creates for financial freedom. You've dipped your toe in the water and tried a micro-investing app. But you're not going to get rich investing in 50-cent increments.

When you want to invest directly in the market, rather than through micro-investing apps, you need a broker.

There are a lot of choices out there, and it can be difficult to decide which one is right for you. Good news—you don't have to make the perfect choice right away.

Firstly, let's understand what a broker is.

What is a broker?

A **broker** is a person or company who acts on your behalf to buy and sell shares through the market. They are your agent, representing you at the stock market and working on your behalf to buy and sell your shares.

PARDON THE JARGON
broker

A **broker** is a person or company that acts on your behalf to buy and sell shares through the market. You place the order, in person, via phone or online, and they will execute the trade for you.

Have you ever been to a house auction and seen someone there on the phone, taking instructions from a bidder on the other end? Think of the person at the auction on the phone as your broker. They're executing your decisions to buy or sell stocks.

If you wanted to buy shares in JB Hi-Fi, for example, you can't just walk up to the front door of their head office and ask to buy some shares. Well, you could, but it would be to no avail, and quite embarrassing.

You need someone to go out there, act on your behalf and find you some JB Hi-Fi shares in the market. Let's say you want to buy 100 shares. You will instruct the broker to go and buy 100 JB Hi-Fi shares. They then go to the market and find someone who is looking to sell 100 JB Hi-Fi shares at the price you want to buy.

Why do you need someone to do that for you? A broker is the middle person between you and everyone else trying to buy and sell a company's shares. It would be very difficult for you to go out onto the street to find someone, by chance, who might want to be selling 100 JB Hi-Fi shares. A broker goes to the market, where there may be thousands of people looking to sell JB Hi-Fi shares at different prices, and finds you the best deal, according to your instructions.

Traditionally, this would have been literally done by a person. Your parents or grandparents would have called their broker, told them to buy some shares, and the broker would have gone to the market to find available shares to buy, from someone willing to sell.

This process was sluggish and expensive. The broker options available to everyday investors were limited, so accessing the market was relatively tricky.

The great news for us though is that brokers have changed with the internet and new technology. Gone are the days of having to make a phone call to place a trade—although you still can if you want. Gone are the days of paying someone exorbitant fees to do it for you.

Now, you can buy and sell as easily as buying shoes online. With the acceleration of the internet and technology, broker platforms have replaced the old-school way of doing things. It's now possible to make investments from your bed, with so much information at your fingertips.

Types of brokers

There are two key types of brokers you need to know about:

1 Personal brokers: stockbrokers who offer you the real deal, all the bells and whistles. You'll either meet them in person or contact them over the phone. They can offer you recommendations, advice and opinions about stocks and companies. They have access to a lot of data, information and analysis that makes the decision to buy or sell easier for you. With personal brokers, they will work with you one on one, so they come to know your investment style and level of risk. These brokers often won't deal with small amounts of money and can be quite expensive. Ultimately the decision to buy and sell is still in your hands.
2 Online brokers: we use online brokers, or platforms as they're now called, and it's where many people now start their investing journey. There are a number of great platforms available online that act as brokers, where you do the buying and selling yourself. Online brokers are cheaper but also require a much more hands-on approach from you.

There is no right or wrong approach here. If you feel like you want to go to the personal route, by all means go for it. If you want to go the cheaper option, and start online, that's equally fine. The main thing is to find what works for you, and makes you feel comfortable. Keep in mind, you're not locked into the first broker you choose. We'll keep saying this. This is not a life sentence; there's no lock-in contract.

Don't let choosing the perfect broker be the barrier that keeps you from starting.

Factors to consider when deciding on a broker

There is not one broker that suits everyone's needs. There's no one-size-fits-all. In fact, we use multiple brokers for different reasons.

Choosing brokers

ALEC
My first broker was CommSec. Since I started my first Dollarmites account at school, I had done all my banking with Commonwealth Bank so it was easy to create an investing account with Commonwealth Bank's broker, CommSec.

Over time, I learnt about other brokers in the market that offered the same service at a cheaper price, so I opened an account with IG Markets. IG was cheaper and offered access to a variety of international markets. Over time even cheaper options came into the market and lowered the cost of investing even further.

Stake offered free brokerage for US stocks, meaning I could buy and sell American companies with no brokerage costs. Superhero offered cheaper access to Australian stocks.

I still have all four brokerage accounts active. My biggest learning over the journey is that there are no switching costs between brokers; it is easy to start another account with another platform. So I did.

For beginner investors, my advice is: don't let perfection be the enemy of the good. When it comes to choosing brokers, you can spend a lot of time trying to find the absolute perfect broker for you. However, I've learnt that it is easy to change. If you start with one option and decide you don't like it, you can move. Just get started!

BRYCE

Like Alec, my first broker was CommSec—Commonwealth Bank's online platform. At the time it was one of the main brokers in the market, along with the other Big 4 banks—ANZ, NAB and Westpac. Given I had a cash account with CommSec, it was an easy way to start.

CommSec provided a lot of resources, from charts to broker reports and research. But it came at a cost. I didn't need all of this additional information. I just wanted to be able to buy and sell. As I progressed, and became more aware of the impact of fees on my investment returns, I decided to have a look at what else was available. More online platforms were coming to the market, and I wanted international exposure. So I signed up to IG and Stake—both platforms providing low, or no, brokerage and also access to international markets.

I still have all platforms active, and use them for different things. My message would be: don't get bogged down in trying to find the perfect one. You can move as your style of investing changes. It is possible to transfer between brokers, so don't let this put you off.

When deciding what broker to go with, there are a number of factors to consider. We've chosen two key factors we think are relevant, and identified what you should be thinking about.

1 Costs

We want to keep our costs as low as possible. Any money that you're paying to a broker is money that isn't going to your investments or into your pocket. Over time, paying too much in costs can really add up. That's why our number one consideration is the fees (as we keep saying!). When it comes to brokers, the biggest cost (or fee) is the cost to buy and sell shares.

This cost is known as **brokerage**.

PARDON THE JARGON
brokerage

Brokerage is the cost a broker charges to buy and sell shares on your behalf.

It can be a flat fee per trade: for example, $5 every time you buy or sell a stock. Or it can be a percentage of the total investment amount: for example, 1% for investments over $5,000 (which would mean if you invested $5,000 you would pay $50).

If you're planning to invest often, then keeping your brokerage as low as possible should be your first consideration. If you're planning to invest infrequently, you should still aim to pay as little as possible. At the end of the day, whether you pay $20 or $5 in brokerage, you are still buying the same stock. Don't pay more than you need to.

All brokers will have their costs available on their websites, so you can find this information before signing up.

2 Overseas markets

Think about some of the brands you use every day. Even just think about your morning run. You pull on Nike clothes (American), Adidas shoes (German), play music from Spotify (Sweden) on your Samsung phone (South Korea). The world is globalised and your investments can be too . . . if you pick the right broker.

It used to be incredibly difficult and expensive to access international markets, like the USA or those in Europe. This was a huge barrier.

The USA is home to the biggest stock market in the world, with some of the world's largest companies. Having easy access to it is so important. Luckily, there are platforms today that give you cheap, easy access to overseas markets.

Not all brokers offer international markets. Some *only* offer international markets. Again, this information will be publicly available on the broker's website, so you can do some research before creating an account.

Can I have more than one broker account?

Yes, you can. There's nothing wrong with having more than one. We have more than one active broker account. It's likely you will too, especially if you're trying to access both domestic and international shares with low fees.

If you grow out of your broker, or a new one comes along that you're more impressed with, there are options for you to move your portfolio across. Your broker should have a form available, often called a broker-to-broker or off-market-transfer form. The broker or custodian will then initiate the transfer request on your behalf. There may be some fees involved, but the main thing to know is that it is possible, so don't let it stop you changing if you want to.

Process of buying and selling with a broker

At this point we're throwing a lot of information your way. Just to sum up where we're at so far:

- You do not need to find someone selling shares yourself; a broker does it for you.
- There are plenty of different options for brokers out there.
- Share prices do not change between brokers.
- You can always change brokers as you learn; don't feel like your first choice has to be a perfect choice when choosing a broker.

You've picked a broker: how does it actually work from here?

Buying shares online works like online shopping. When you're buying something online, you search for it and then click the 'buy' button. It's the same with online brokers. You search for the stock you want to buy, click the 'buy' button and then the broker will go out and buy it for you.

At this stage, we want to introduce the idea of **stock tickers**. These tickers are how you search for stocks on the broker's website.

PARDON THE JARGON
stock ticker

Most companies listed on a stock market have a three- or four-digit code that they are identified by, which is called a **stock ticker**. Companies will often be referred to by their stock market tickers. For example, Afterpay may be referred to as APT or Woolworths may be referred to as WOW.

To find out a company's stock ticker, you can simply google it or look on the company's website.

Here are a few examples of some of Australia's most famous companies and their stock tickers.

- Afterpay (APT)
- Coles (COL)
- Commonwealth Bank (CBA)
- Domino's Pizza (DMP)
- Macquarie Group (MQG)
- National Australia Bank (NAB)
- Qantas Airways (QAN)
- Seek (SEK)
- Sydney Airport (SYD)
- Telstra (TLS)
- Woolworths (WOW).

Everything you need to know, and a lot you might want to

To start your investing journey, this is about as much as you really need to consider. You'll learn the rest as you go. You could live a long and happy life without worrying about access to live data or having the most up-to-date technology at your fingertips.

You are not locked into the first broker you sign up to. Don't make finding the perfect one the barrier that stops you starting.

But, if you want to know more and understand some of the 'juicy' elements of brokers, continue reading . . .

Everything you may, one day, want to know about brokers

Information-overload alert! The most common type of question we get here at Equity Mates is on brokers. So we didn't want to write a book without covering everything we've learnt about brokers. For some readers, this may feel unnecessary—feel free to skip over these grey pages. Just remember you can always refer back to this section if you ever have a question about brokers during your investing journey.

There are a number of other factors that you might want to consider when researching brokers. Each of them will have a different level of importance depending on the type of investor you are.

This may seem like a lot of jargon, and information. Don't feel like you need to understand it all. As you progress with your journey, some factors may become more relevant.

Here are the factors to consider when searching for a broker.

Costs

We mentioned before we want to keep our costs as low as possible. Some key tips to think about:

- Each broker charges different fees, with online platforms providing the cheapest options.

- Brokerage may change depending on where you are buying your stocks: i.e., are you buying Australian companies or international companies? Choose a platform that will give you the cheapest option for the area you want to buy. This may mean you need to have more than one broker.
- Some platforms charge based on how often you are investing per month. Be careful with this. If you don't plan to buy frequently, then make sure you won't be penalised for not investing monthly.
- The size of your trades can determine how much you pay in brokerage. Some platforms have an investment-value threshold that, if you exceed, you pay a percentage rather than a flat fee. While it might be irrelevant when you're first starting and investing small amounts, it is something to be aware of.

Other fees to be mindful of:
- Subscription services: for a monthly fee, some platforms are now offering a subscription service, where you get additional benefits, cheaper (or no) brokerage, and other bells and whistles. If you go down this path, make sure you take the time to do some quick calculations—will the monthly fee be worth it given how often you plan to invest?
- Foreign exchange: some brokers will charge a foreign exchange conversion on deposits and withdrawals. This means they're taking a clip when you change your Australian dollars (AUD) into United States dollars (USD), for example. This is only applicable if you're buying stocks in the USA, and the broker uses USD.

 LISTENER QUESTION
how much should I pay for brokerage?

As little as possible!

To be more specific, our general rule of thumb is to try to keep your brokerage below 1% of your investment amount. Here are a few examples:

- Broker A charges $5 per trade. That means you want to be investing $500 or more
- Broker B charges $9.50 per trade. That means you want to be investing $950 or more.
- Broker C charges $19.95 per trade. That means you want to be investing $1,950 or more.

Handy tip: Brokerage of $2 might seem cheap but if you're only investing $50, this means you're paying 4%!

Overseas markets

Don't confine your universe to the domestic market. Choosing a broker that offers access to overseas markets will expand your options.

Some key tips to think about:

- Compare the number of global markets each platform allows you to access.
- Some platforms are domestic only.
- Some platforms are international only.
- Check the brokerage for international shares—it varies significantly between platforms.
- Compare the number of stocks and exchange-traded funds (ETFs) available on international markets: for example, some platforms don't offer you everything that is listed on the S&P 500 in the USA.
- Check what currency is required to invest—some brokers will convert your AUD into other currencies.

Market data

There is no shortage of data when it comes to investing. You'll be able to find data on almost anything, and use it in very creative ways to build your investing strategy. Many platforms use data as a way to differentiate themselves from the competition. We would encourage you, firstly, not to get overwhelmed by the data. You don't need to know what it all means when you first start.

Secondly, our rule of thumb is that the more you pay for a broker, generally the more comprehensive and 'live' the data will be. What do we mean by 'live'? The ASX feeds data out during trading hours that platforms use. This includes the latest stock prices, the volume of trades (how many stocks have been bought or sold), company announcements—you name it. Depending on your platform, this data can be delayed, in some cases by up to 20 minutes.

If you're looking to invest for the long term, then this shouldn't matter too much. If you're thinking about day trading, then you will need a platform that provides 'live' data.

Some key things to think about:

- Will you be able to access static, live, dynamic or real-time data, and does this attract any extra fees?
- Does the platform provide data on the company's key metrics?
- Does it provide historical financial information on companies?
- Does it have basic or comprehensive charting options?

Order options

There are many ways in which you can buy and sell a stock in the market or, in other words, place an order. For example, you can let the forces of supply and demand work, and let the market determine the price at which you buy or sell your stock. This is called a 'market order'. Or, you can be more specific and tell the market you only want to buy at a specific price. This is called a 'limit order'.

For now, you just need to be aware that not all brokers offer the same amount of order types. When you're first starting out, you probably won't need a huge variety of order types, as it can get a little tricky and feel overwhelming and confusing. As you progress and become more confident, different order types may become important.

Some key things to think about:

- What orders would I like to have available?
- What order options do the various brokers offer?
- Can you place limit and market orders?
- Are stop-loss orders available to help you minimise investment losses?
- When are the orders executed?

Navigation and execution

Some platforms look like they haven't been upgraded since 1980, and others resemble the sleek, easy-to-use apps that we're accustomed to in the 21st century. The good news is that most are free to sign up to, and some even provide a demo account. You can try before you buy! There's no harm in signing up to a few you think you might like to use and having a look around.

Some key things to consider:

- Is the platform easy to navigate, and does it make sense?
- Do you like the look and feel?
- Is it simple to place trades and get an update on your portfolio performance?

Access

Accessing your portfolio when and how you want might be important to you. There are many ways that you can place trades and get market information.

Some key things to consider:

- As well as an online platform, can you place trades over the phone or on the go using a smartphone or tablet app?
- Is the trading system a web-based platform or does it require you to download any software?

Customer support

When you're first starting out, sometimes it's easier to speak to someone to get assistance. Having access to customer support could mean the difference between you placing a trade the right way, and placing it the wrong way (and losing out!)

Some key things to think about:

- Make sure you can easily contact the share trading platform provider if you ever have a question about your account or a problem with a trade.
- Look for phone, email and live chat support, as well as online learning centres and education tools.

Community

Another way that platforms try to differentiate themselves is to offer the opportunity to be part of a community. If you're looking to learn from other investors, compare yourself to others, see what others are buying and selling, then there are platforms that will give you this opportunity. But be careful—blindly following others does have its downsides. Ensure that you're joining the community for the right reasons, and do your own research!

> It is important to remember you're not locked in to any one broker. You don't pay to sign up, so you can sign up to and try different platforms before settling on the one you prefer.

Terms you need to know, but not really . . .

Forgive us if the next little section is a little dry, but there are some important, and common, terms that you will come across when setting up your broker, and buying and selling shares. These are worth discussing, as they can be confusing, and some of them do divide opinion.

Share registry

A share registry is a company that is between you and the company you have invested in. Listed companies have thousands of shareholders, so it would be awfully time consuming for them to manage all of the personal details and share ownership details of all their investors.

This is the role of the share registry. It works on behalf of the listed company to manage the company's shareholder information and correspondence. Share registries in Australia include Link Market Services, Computershare and Boardroom Pty Ltd.

Registries are where you go to update your personal information, and your dividend preferences among other things. This is important so you can get paid your dividends from the company you're invested in! It is possible for you to have accounts with multiple share registries, depending on how many stocks you own.

Just a word of warning—the ASX loves sending paperwork, and you'll receive it through your share registry.

Issuer-sponsored shares

Issuer-sponsored shares are issued to you directly from the company, or managed directly by the issuer, through their share registry. These shares can still be traded through a broker.

How do you know if it's an issuer-sponsored share? The shares are allocated a security reference number (SRN). You will see this SRN acronym, and then generally a number starting with the letter I, on the paperwork you receive from the ASX.

CHESS

Clearance House Electronic Subregister System—the computer system used by the Australian Securities Exchange (ASX) to record shareholdings and manage all of the transaction settlements.

CHESS-sponsored shares

Otherwise known as broker-sponsored shares, CHESS-sponsored shares are issued via CHESS, and sponsored by your stockbroker or investment platform. In other words, CHESS means that the ASX is keeping records of who owns what shares and when. CHESS is the most common way of people buying and selling.

CHESS-sponsored shares are identified by a holder identification number (HIN) that usually starts with an X. This is the number that links the holdings back to you. You can have multiple HINs if you use a number of different brokers. If you move brokers, you can move your HIN and the shares attached to it.

In both instances—issuer-sponsored and CHESS-sponsored shares—there are two things to keep in mind:

1　When you buy a stock you don't get to choose if it's CHESS or issuer, but you don't need to worry about it.
2　You own the stocks directly—no one else is holding them on your behalf.

Custodian

To keep fees low, there are a number of brokers and online platforms that use a custodian model. Simply put, this means when you purchase shares through your platform, your shares are then held by a regulated custodian, rather than you directly.

Don't panic. You still have claim and beneficial ownership of your shares. It's just a different model. Shares under a custodian model are still also registered through CHESS.

You will hear some people say there is a risk that if your broker goes under you will lose your stocks. These shares are held by custodians (a separate company to your broker) so you will still get your shares should something happen to your broker.

The nuts and bolts of buying and selling

We've gone through the initial stages of building the foundations, and getting started. We've discussed the concept of starting small. We've talked about buying the index, we've looked at brokers, and outlined ways to find your first individual company to invest in.

Now it's down to the nuts and bolts, and it's time to press the 'buy' button. Here are some important pieces of information to consider.

A step-by-step guide on how to buy and sell your shares

By this stage you've likely jumped the gun, and perhaps gone and bought your first shares. Epic! Keep reading. If you haven't yet pulled the trigger, perhaps you've found a broker and have had a look around. Don't panic if you haven't, there's time for that later.

We get a lot of questions around 'order types' when people first start, and this can be very confusing if you don't know what you're doing.

Let's strip the process of buying a stock right back to the basics.

You've got $500 to buy your first investment. Through your online platform, you search the ASX code, or stock ticker, for the stock. For example, if you want to buy Afterpay, its ticker code is APT. Type that code in, and your stock will come up, along with the option to buy or sell.

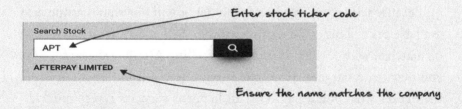

Click on the 'buy' button, and you'll be presented with a number of options.

You need to decide if you are going to buy a specific *quantity* of shares, or a *dollar value* of shares. If you went in with the idea to invest $500, then you'd be going for the dollar value.

When you enter $500, the broker will work out how many shares you can buy for the amount. If the shares are $10, you'll be able to buy 50 shares.

If the shares are $9, you'll be able to buy 55 shares. If your broker doesn't let you buy fractions of shares, then you will have $5 left from your $500 ($500/$9 = 55.5 shares—but you can't buy 0.5 of a share, so you'll get 55).

Keep in mind, if you only have $500, and brokerage is $10, you really only have $490 to invest. Many people often forget this and wonder why their full $500 was not invested.

If you choose to order based on quantity instead of value, you just need to make sure you have enough money in your broker account to pay for it. For example, say you want 100 APT stocks. Let's say it's trading at $90 per share—you're going to need $9,000 plus brokerage.

Back to the $500 example. You've told your broker you want $500 worth of APT. The default will generally be what's called a 'market' order. This is where you press 'buy' but you don't have strict control over the price you buy it. Afterpay might be trading at $90 when you click the buy button. What happens in the background is your order for $500 worth of shares is sent out into the market, to find someone selling $500 worth of shares.

Because you've put in a 'market' order, it will buy shares at the next available price. This could mean it's at $90, $89 or $91. It's whatever can be matched with a seller. If someone is selling Afterpay shares for $40, you may get a bargain. If no one is willing to sell for less than $100, then that's what you'll pay. This all happens very, very, very quickly.

Why would you do a market order? If you want to buy the stock as fast as possible, and don't really care about a few cents difference here or there, then it's the easiest and quickest way to buy (or sell) your stocks.

Once you hit 'buy', your order is sent off into the market to be matched with a seller. When a match is found, the order will execute and your newly bought shares will appear in your portfolio.

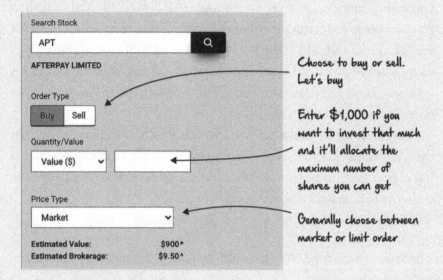

Search Stock

APT

AFTERPAY LIMITED

Order Type

Buy | Sell

Choose to buy or sell. Let's buy

Quantity/Value

Value ($)

Enter $1,000 if you want to invest that much and it'll allocate the maximum number of shares you can get

Price Type

Market

Generally choose between market or limit order

Estimated Value: $900*
Estimated Brokerage: $9.50^

The different types of orders

We've mentioned 'market' orders but there are a couple of other order types to know about.

1 Limit order

As the name suggests, this is where you put a limit on the price you are willing to buy or sell. Let's say you want to buy $500 worth of APT, but only for $90 or cheaper. If it's currently trading at $95, your order will sit in the market until there is someone willing to sell you $500 worth at $90 or cheaper. If there is no one to buy from, your order won't get filled. A buy limit sets the maximum price you're prepared to pay.

Additionally, you can put a limit on when you sell. For example, you bought APT, and it went up to $105. You put a sell order in, but for nothing less than $100. This means it will sell your shares if it matches an order between $100 and $105. A sell limit sets the minimum price you're willing to sell for.

2 Stop-loss order

A stop-loss is an order you put in to protect your downside, to prevent you losing money. Let's say you bought APT for $90. You can then place an order to instruct the broker to sell if it drops to $80. The order will sit there, and will trigger if the price hits $80. The advantage of using a stop-loss is you don't have to worry about keeping an eye on your stocks all the time. You can use this order type to cut your losses quickly and move on.

Caveat though—if the price drops too quickly, it can shoot through the $80 so quickly that your order won't be filled. A stop-loss order is not a guarantee to sell at the price you want. Not all brokers offer the stop-loss functionality either.

Let's pause and cap off what we just discussed.

There are three types of main orders you will come across: market, limit, stop-loss.

- Market: the market will match the price for you, and this generally happens very quickly.
- Limit: you set a maximum price at which you're willing to buy, or a minimum at which you're willing to sell.
- Stop-loss: after purchasing your shares, you set a price at which you would like your stocks to automatically sell.

Your order isn't working

Don't worry; this is unlikely to be your fault.

Sometimes orders aren't filled because there is literally no one on the other side of the trade able to sell you the shares at the price you want, when you want. For a market order, this is unlikely, but for limit, it can happen. Just know that you haven't done anything wrong. You may need to adjust the order if you're desperate to buy the stock.

When can I buy and sell?

The Australian Securities Exchange (ASX) is open from 10 a.m. to 4 p.m., Monday to Friday, and does not open on public holidays. Seriously cruisy—not your average 9–5!

Your window to place trades is not limited to the time but your orders won't be executed outside those times. Say you get home from work, you haven't had a chance to look at the markets but you want to buy some stocks. It's 8.30 p.m.

Can you place an order out of hours?

Yes, but your order will sit in the queue until the market opens at 10 a.m. the next day. Then it'll go into the open market to try to find a match.

Be careful though. If you've placed a 'market' order, at say $7 for Kogan shares, the stock might open the next day at $8.50 off the back of some really positive sales news from Kogan the night before. Where you thought you'd be buying around $7, you could be matched much closer to $8.50.

Do the order types really matter?

It depends on what you're trying to achieve. If you're day trading, or short-term trading, then buying and selling at precise prices certainly makes a difference, and cutting your losses quickly is important. Knowing your order types and how to execute properly are worth it.

If you have a long-term view of investing, our opinion is that a stock at $10 is probably still a good investment at $10.25. Our margin of error is not so thin that the ordinary movement of the market—day in, day out—should move it from a good investment to a bad one.

Because of this, we're personally more open to using market orders and placing orders outside market hours, given we can't keep an eye on the market all day.

TL;DR—what does this all really mean?

It may seem like there is a lot to consider when looking for a broker. To make it easy for you:

- Don't let finding 'the perfect one' stop you from getting started.
- You can chop and change as you progress on your journey (and transfer your stocks between brokers with ease).
- Try to keep your fees as low as possible and get international exposure.

For a lot of everyday people, choosing the right broker is where they decide investing is too hard. One of the biggest things we've learnt over the Equity Mates journey is that, even if you make the absolute worst choice here, it's still better than nothing. Whatever broker you choose, it's worth it to get started investing.

Finding the right investing information

There is so much information out there that it can become
overwhelming. Finding good sources of information, and removing
the noise, goes a long way to helping you keep calm and focused
on your investing goal.

In a world of 24/7 news cycles, social media, and smartphones, there
is a lot of information to consume. A lot of it, though, is just noise.
What do we mean by noise? It's unwanted, unnecessary information
that only disrupts and clouds your longer-term thinking.

A lot of the financial news and information you see is based on the
here and now. What did markets do today? Which companies went
up? Which went down? How will the market react tomorrow?

These are all valid things to report on but do they really make a
difference to your investing strategy? News headlines can change their
opinion in a matter of days. If you based your investing decisions on
the latest click-bait title, you'd be trading in and out of positions faster
than you can blink an eye.

Removing the noise and concentrating on information that is going
to help you make long-term decisions is an important skill to develop.
Don't get us wrong—it's hard to do! Browsing social media, scrolling
through news sites—we all generally do it.

Having a few go-to sources of investing information will really help
you to develop some clear thinking, and identify what is noise and
what is useful.

The perils of the sensationalist headline

News is designed to be sensational. It's designed to draw you in and sell more papers, get more clicks and win as much attention as possible. Getting sucked into the day-to-day noise can be a killer for investing success.

Some of the best companies in the world have thrived despite negative headlines day after day. There is no clearer example of this than Tesla, the electric car company started by Elon Musk.

Here we've put Tesla's share price with just a handful of the negative headlines Tesla has enjoyed over the years.

Tesla—a great company with terrible press

Tesla has been a public company for a little over 10 years. In that time, it has risen over 15,000%. Meaning every $1 invested has turned into over $150!

This is despite some terrible headlines for the company in this time:

'Tesla's Struggles Raise Questions About Electric Cars', *The New York Times*, 25 September 2012

'Tesla Motors' Dirty Little Secret is a Major Problem', Motley Fool, 19 January 2014

'Musk's Master Plan for Tesla is a Master Spin Job', *Industry Week*, 13 July 2016

'Tesla Factory Workers Reveal Pain, Injury and Stress: "Everything Feels Like the Future But Us"', *The Guardian*, 18 May 2017

'Tesla Suffers Its Worst Day of the Year After Brutal Earnings Report and Loss of Technology Chief', CNBC, 25 July 2019

All of these news stories looked bad for Tesla at the time, but it continued growing and in hindsight a lot of these headlines haven't mattered. Investors who sold because of the day-to-day news would have missed the longer term story that Tesla was building.

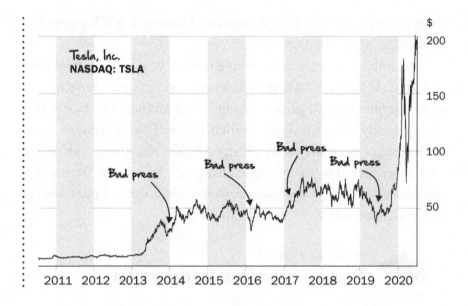

Tesla, Inc.
NASDAQ: TSLA

Bad press

Bad press

Bad press

Bad press

How we find information

We both read broadly. Warren Buffett says to 'read 500 pages . . . every day. That's how knowledge works. It builds up, like compound interest. All of you can do it, but I guarantee not many of you will do it.'

He's right on two fronts. Firstly, reading a lot, and often, is a game changer. It exposes you to so many different ideas and ways of thinking. Some of the best investors in the world have written books rich with information. You don't need a degree to be an investor. Anyone can do it. Start upskilling yourself. We'd suggest trying to read five investing books. We've listed some of our favourites at the end of Part 9.

Secondly, 500 pages a day?! He's got to be joking. Who has time for that?! We'd encourage you to read when you can, as much as you can. Don't stress yourself out trying to pump through books for the sake of it. Take your time. Absorb what they're saying.

Traditional financial media also play a pretty big part in our information universe. There are a number of quality publications that do great reporting on the business and economic environment. Some of them do require a monthly subscription. Sometimes it is better to pay for quality, to remove that noise.

The internet has created a whole culture of sharing information and ideas. If you know where to look, you can engage in some quality conversations that will propel your investing journey. The best part is that generally this sort of information is free. From forums to social media groups, there are plenty of opportunities to connect with people with experience. They're willing to share their knowledge, from which you can learn a hell of a lot. Again, we've shared some of our favourite online destinations at the end of this chapter.

 FROM THE EXPERTS
finding investing information

Nick Cregan is a partner and portfolio manager of Fairlight Asset Management. We asked him what his go-to source was for investing information:

> 'We lean really heavily on the literature that's actually produced directly by the companies. Annual reports, quarterly releases, conference notes, proxy statements—it might be boring, but we find that collating the information from the source, rather than relying on brokers or blogs or other authors out there helps us form independent views. And I think that independent views are critically important if you want to avoid making investing mistakes.
>
> We do also try to speak to management to glean some insights regarding culture and strategy. I know that's not available to everyone, but it's something that's been pretty important to our process.
>
> I'd definitely read as many of the investor letters out there. So, if you go to the 13F filings* that you can find, and letters that are put out over time, you can really come across some interesting things.
>
> And then the usual suspects in terms of financial press is a good place to understand sort of what's happening from a strategy point of view. So we read the *Financial Times*, *The Wall Street Journal*, the usual suspects, but there's nothing proprietary in that. But being broadly informed is a very good place to be.'

---

* A 13F filing is a compulsory quarterly report in the USA, filed by fund managers who manage $100 million or more, that lists their US investments.

Sources of information to consider

Once you've found a company you may be interested in, it's then important to go and do further research to form a view about the company.
There are some great tools out there to help you do this.

- **Company annual reports**: each publicly listed company is required
  to produce an annual report that details everything from its financial performance through to its strategy for the coming years. It's
  a fantastic resource to get a lot of specific information about the
  company. The reports can be long and sometimes there will be
  sections that you don't understand but each report will have an
  executive summary that at least you should read. The reports can
  be found on the ASX website, through your brokerage platform or
  on the company's website.
- **Google/Yahoo Finance**: Google and Yahoo both provide great
  financial information about listed companies. All you need to do
  is type in the ASX code for the company and away you go. The
  information is presented in an easy-to-read format and is often our
  first stop when we want to find out the latest financial information
  about a company.
- **Your broker platform**: your brokerage platform is a fantastic place
  to start getting specific information about your company. It will have
  ratings, archives of annual reports, financial information, as well as
  information on competitors and the industry. It's worth noting that
  not all brokers provide this level of information.
- **Daily news:** almost everything that you read in the news can
  have an impact on your investing decisions. Try to be aware of
  opportunities when reading the news. For example, a cyclone up in
  Queensland can have a huge impact on companies, both positively
  and negatively. Insurance companies, building and construction,
  agriculture and retail will all be affected by the cyclone. Try to
  think how it will affect them and what it would mean from an
  investing point of view.

- **Social media**: social media is a fantastic source of up-to-date information about what is trending now. Investors love to share their advice, thoughts, and latest finds. Businesses use social media to spread information as well, so it can often be a great place to start looking for opportunities and getting ideas.
- **Investor communities and forums:** these are fantastic sources of information. You will find a lot of hidden gems in communities online, as investors share their latest finds, hot tips and tricks. It is very important to remember when you are reading through communities and forums that you form your own opinions, and don't take others' words as gospel.

 FROM THE EXPERTS

the benefits of Twitter

Tobias Carlisle is the founder and managing director of Acquirers Funds LLC. We asked him what his go-to source was for investing information:

'I love Twitter. I can't go past Twitter. It's sort of become an indispensable tool for what I do.

If you follow the right people, the information flow is incredible and you get it hours before it appears on the television. I don't have CNBC on in the office or anything like that. I just have Twitter. And if you follow a mix of guys who are reporters and other investors and analysts, you get information as it's delivered and then you get analysis of that information. I find it's a really great way of knowing what is happening.

Cliff Asness runs a $200 billion firm. He's a billionaire. He's got a PhD, he worked at Goldman Sachs. And he's been running this firm for twenty years. He's on Twitter and you can interact with him. Jim O'Shaughnessy is on Twitter. He runs O'Shaughnessy Asset Management, [a] similar multibillion-dollar firm, and they will talk to you. If you're polite and you've got a sensible, good question for them, they will respond. I just think Twitter is phenomenal. That's really the thing that I would recommend to everybody.'

Key tips we've picked up related to investing information

With a lot of information out there, it can be hard to make heads or tails of it. Here are some of the key lessons we've learned:

- Be careful of too much information—it can paralyse your decision making.
- Headlines are designed to be sensationalist. Your portfolio is designed for the long term.
- Ask yourself: is this short-term news? Will it matter in twelve months? Will it matter in five years?
- Stories are great, but data is compelling. Ensure you're getting a good mix of both sides.

It's as easy as E-T-F

Picking stocks is daunting. The fear of having to pick one or two, with the hope their prices will go up, is a barrier for many people. That's why exchange-traded funds (ETFs) have become such a popular investment product.

ETFs first appeared as investment products in 1989, and have since become wildly popular among all types of investors. Globally, ETFs are forecast to reach a total market capitalisation of US$25 trillion by 2027.

Today, ETFs are one of the most popular products used by beginners. They are a great way to gain access to a number of companies in one simple trade.

What are exchange-traded funds?

Let's start at the top. You've probably heard about **ETFs** a lot (we've even mentioned them a few times already). They're the investment product of choice for many people. More and more are becoming available on the market, giving people easy, simple ways to get exposure to many different companies and asset classes.

 PARDON THE JARGON
ETFs

ETF is one of the most common acronyms you'll come across as an investor. It stands for exchange-traded fund. ETFs are a common investing option that allow you to buy a group of stocks in one trade.

There are two elements to ETFs:

1. Exchange-traded: they are traded on a stock exchange, such as the ASX, allowing you to buy and sell them like you would a share.
2. Fund: they are funds that are managed by professional investors.

In a nutshell, ETFs allow you to buy and sell units of a professionally managed fund in the same way you'd buy and sell shares in a single company.

ETFs are investment funds that are traded on an exchange, just like any normal share. The process of buying an ETF is exactly the same as the process of buying an individual company.

As you're buying into a fund, you are getting exposure to a variety of stocks. This provides opportunity for diversification, access to different asset classes, through a single trade.

To put it all together, an ETF is an investment product that is traded on an exchange, just like any normal stock, that gives you access to a range of different stocks in one trade.

What does that mean?

If you've got $1,000 to invest in American stocks, you don't have to choose between Nike, Disney, Apple, Amazon, Lululemon and Tesla. Instead you can invest a little bit in all of them. In one trade you can invest in a fund that holds all the biggest American stocks, giving you access to all of these stocks and more.

Sounds awesome, right? It is! We hope you're starting to see how ETFs are a great way to start your investing journey.

Let's expand on this in some more detail, as it's important to understand.

How do ETFs work?

One of the main reasons ETFs are so popular is that they're built to give you broad exposure to a number of different stocks. The outcome of this is you get the overall return of all the stocks in the

ETF. We've spoken about indexes in Part 5, and this is where ETFs come into play.

The most common ETFs track an index. For example, you might want to get exposure to the Australian ASX 200 index—the top 200 companies in Australia. You could go out and buy all 200 individually. You would probably have to take out a mortgage to afford it! Or you could buy an ETF that tracks this ASX 200 index.

In one easy trade, you can buy an ETF that holds all 200 companies and, on that basis, you get to own them all. The performance of the ETF is based on the collective performance of the index, or all 200 stocks.

We'll use an analogy of a fruit salad to explain how it all works.

Let's assume a bunch of fruit—bananas, apples, mangos, oranges and peaches—represent the top five companies in Australia. Before ETFs, if you want to own all five, you would have to buy each individually. A full banana, a full apple etc. This is an expensive option.

An ETF is a proverbial fruit salad. Rather than having to buy a full banana and a full apple, you can buy a fruit salad that has a little bit of all of this fruit. You get a slice of each fruit, all packed up together for your convenience.

You take the pre-packed fruit salad through the checkout and you're on your way. It's a cheaper and more convenient way to get a bit of each of the fruits you're after.

An ETF operates the same way. The ETF packages up a slice of each company and lets you buy it in one easy transaction. It saves you having to choose between bananas and mangos and you can get a taste of everything. Easy!

Passive index tracking

Most ETFs are passively managed. This means there's no one buying and selling every day, no one making decisions. If it says it's going to track the ASX 200 index, it's going to track that index. It doesn't matter if the price is going up or down.

!&?# PARDON THE JARGON
passive versus active management

Two terms you'll come across as an investor are **active management** and **passive management**. These are different approaches fund managers take when investing your money.

Active management is where the investor is making decisions about what to buy and sell. They are trying to use their knowledge and insight to buy the right stocks at the right time to get the best return.

Passive management is where the investor is not making decisions about what to buy and sell. Instead, they follow a set of rules and just hold whatever stocks the rules dictate, regardless of the performance of these stocks. Passive funds are usually designed to follow a particular stock market or industry.

With **passive management** there is no one picking individual stocks to try to outperform the market. These ETFs hold all of the stocks that are in a particular index, and aim to give the investor the returns of the overall index.

If we were to build on the fruit salad analogy: the ETF will have a bit of apple, banana, pear etc. It will track the price of this basket of fruit. There is no one chopping and changing different fruit. No one is saying bananas are getting too expensive, so let's sell them and replace them with kiwi fruit. The ETF simply tracks the price of all the fruit in the bowl, regardless of how each type of fruit is performing.

It is the same for these index-tracking ETFs. If an ASX 200 ETF holds Westpac stock, it will continue to hold Westpac stock. It doesn't matter if the CEO says something embarrassing at a press conference, the Australian housing market collapses or a string of bank robberies leaves them high and dry. The ETF will continue holding whatever stocks are in the index and just track their price.

Why would you do this, you may ask. Surely you want someone actively managing the account to ensure that these bad stocks, this rotten fruit, is cut out of the fund.

What history has shown us, over and over again, is that most actively managed funds struggle to beat the overall market. Stock market indexes are filled with some of the very best companies, managed by the very best people, and they grow year after year at a good rate (in Australia, the average since 1900 has been 13% per year). History shows it is difficult for a lot of active managers to beat the return of the market over a long period of time.

People are not great judges of the future. We often buy the wrong things and sell at the wrong time. Being passive protects us from ourselves. Over time, it has shown to be a great option for building wealth.

ETFs: the biggest investing trend in the past decade

ETFs have exploded in popularity over the past few decades. The 2010s were a particularly good decade for ETFs. In 2010, there was less than $1 trillion invested in ETFs; by 2020, the amount invested was over $3 trillion!

A huge amount of money has been invested in ETFs over the past decade. Here are a few reasons why.

Equity Mates official policy: we hate fees

ETFs are a very cost-effective way to access the market.

Firstly, buying individual stocks can really add up in terms of brokerage. ETFs give you access to many stocks in one trade, reducing your cost to invest.

Secondly, the management fees are generally a lot lower than other fund options on the market. Because they are set up to passively track an index or asset, there are no active **management fees** charged.

PARDON THE JARGON
management fee

The price charged by the fund manager to invest your money and manage the fund is the **management fee**.

For example, you could buy the A200 ETF, provided by BetaShares, which gives exposure to the top 200 companies in Australia. It has a management fee (the providers need to keep the lights on somehow) of 0.07%.

What does this mean? For every $1,000 you invest, you will only pay $0.70 per year in fees. $0.70! That is ultra-low!

Compare that with another 'actively' managed fund on the market, which charges 1.5% to manage the fund and gives the same exposure. In this instance, for every $1,000 you invest, you'd be paying $15 per year in fees.

You can now see how ETFs are set up to be a cost-effective way to invest in the market.

For every index, there are a number of different companies that offer funds that track the index. When deciding between them, the most important thing to look at is the fees. Why pay more fees for the same product?

You can check the fees on the relevant company's website. They are usually expressed as a percentage, and the lower the percentage, the lower the fees.

Example 1: ASX 200 Index Fund Options (as of December 2020)

Company	Betashares	Vanguard	VanEck	SPDR	iShares
Stock Ticker	A200	VAS	MVW	STW	IOZ
Fees	0.07%	0.10%	0.35%	0.19%	0.09%

Example 2: S&P 500 Index Fund Options (as of December 2020)

Company	iShares*	iShares*	SPDR	ANZ
Stock Ticker	IVV	IHVV	SPY	ZYUS
Fees	0.07%	0.13%	0.09%	0.35%

* What's the difference between these two iShares funds? One is in US Dollars (IVV) and the other is Australian dollars (IHVV).

By choosing one of each of these index funds, you now own a little bit of 200 Australian companies and 500 American companies. You've now truly begun your investing journey.

Why else are ETFs so popular?

If you're still not sold on the idea of ETFs and why they are a great way to start your investing journey, then here are some further advantages to consider.

No stock picking required

- One ETF = access to many stocks.
- There's no need to stress about which stock to pick.

Access

- Traded on stock exchanges, so easy to access them.
- Can buy through your broker, just like any other stock.
- Buy and sell with the click of a button.

Liquidity

Whenever you buy an investment, you want to make sure you can sell it. ETFs are built so you can sell them whenever the market is open, at whatever the market price is that day. No getting stuck with a dud investment!

Flexibility and choice

- There's likely to be an ETF to match your investing goal.
- Hundreds available in Australia, and thousands on markets around the world.
- Choose between countries, industries or asset classes.

Diversification

- In one trade, you get ownership of many companies.
- Reduce your risk in your portfolio by owning companies around the world.
- You get access to not only stocks but other asset classes such as gold, bonds and currency.

What are the risks of investing in ETFs?

The main risk to consider is the investment risk of the underlying asset class of your ETF. The risk is not the product itself, it is what you're investing in. For example, if you buy an ETF that tracks the performance of the gold price, then you're exposing yourself to the risks associated with buying gold.

Similarly, if you buy an ETF that tracks the S&P 500 then you're going to experience movements up and down that will impact the performance of your ETF.

With so many ETFs available, it feels like I'm picking stocks—how should my ETF process begin?

FROM THE EXPERTS

how to choose an ETF

Ilan Israelstam is co-founder and head of strategy and marketing at BetaShares, one of Australia's leading providers of ETFs. Previously, Ilan worked for Boston Consulting Group (BCG), one of the leading global strategy consulting firms. This excerpt comes from a live Q&A we held with Ilan.

Equity Mates: 'This question is coming from one of our listeners and they ask—"Given how many ETFs are available, it can sometimes feel like picking stocks. How do you think about starting your process of choosing ETFs from the many that are available?"'

Ilan: 'It's a great question and I can understand why, with 240 ETFs in Australia [at the time of writing], you could be pretty bamboozled by choice. In that regard, I guess it is like picking stocks, right?

What I would say is because ETFs are generally quite diversified, there is actually quite a big difference between buying ETFs and buying stocks, which means that in most part, the ETF you buy will be quite safe, relatively speaking, compared to buying a single share.

But when you start, I think it's always useful to ask yourself, "why am I investing in the first place?" I imagine that for most people, you're probably trying to save up for something, maybe a deposit for a house or just develop a bit of a nest egg. And what that really means is that for those people, it might be the case that what they're really trying to do is build asset value or build capital over time. We call that "capital growth", in investment land.

So, if that's the case, then there'll be certain types of ETFs that are more aligned with adding to your capital growth over time. And those are typically shares-based ETFs. Shares typically are known to be an asset class which aim to grow capital over time. And that would also mean that, for example, you may not be that focused on generating an income out of this investment because you might be getting paid a salary at your job.

So, hypothetically, what that means is that you'd rather put money into something that will grow over time. So that's an example of making a decision as to why do I want to invest, and will also sculpt the types of ETFs you will be likely to look it.

Then you think about "how long am I going to invest for?" Is this a tactical, or short-term investment? Is this a buy and hold investment I'm trying to make over the long term? Do I want to add to it every month, every fortnight?

Again, if that's the case, you have to ask yourself, "where does this investment fit into the rest of my investment portfolio?" Is the investment being made to become the core of your portfolio, which grows over time? Or, perhaps you've actually already invested in a few Australian shares and you want to diversify by getting some international ETFs, for example.

So with all investments, including of course ETF investments, you have to work out why you're making the investment. Once you have done that, with the large array of options available to investors there is likely going to be an ETF that fits that purpose.

So, to put all this into practice, if I'm just looking to get started in the market, maybe I'll just buy a couple of very simple exchange-traded funds that are passively managed, very broad market indices (indexes) like NASDAQ 100 (NDQ), or Australia 200 (A200) or MSCI World, or S&P 500. These are names of indices which provide exposure to the US, Australia or the world.

And then on the other hand, I might be looking to do something more tactical because I really like the particular theme. An example might be that I am particularly interested in Robotics and Artificial Intelligence. In that case I might take a look at RBTZ for example. The point is that there's enough there to make those decisions—you just have to know yourself and work it out.

So I think, first of all, the process is to understand yourself. Once you've understood yourself, work out if it's shares versus bonds versus whatever you are looking to invest in. Work out whether you want Australian or international exposures, then you would usually try to pick something that's quite broad, unless you're trying to be tactical about it, in which case, by all means, it might make sense to go for something more narrow. But, above all, before making any investment at all, it's important to make sure you understand what's inside that ETF.'

How to buy and sell ETFs

As we touched on earlier, one key advantage of ETFs is the ability to buy and sell them like any normal stock on the stock exchange. This simply means, you buy and sell them through your broker or online trading platform.

All ETFs come with a stock ticker, just like normal stocks. Some of them can be quite creative! For example, there's one available in Australia called HACK, which gives investors exposure to the cyber-security sector.

Strategies

Investing using ETFs opens up a range of different strategies that you could use. We've listed some ways you can think about using ETFs in your investing journey.

Entire portfolio

One approach could be to build a portfolio entirely made up of ETFs. There is nothing wrong with this. You might not have the time required, or the expertise, to focus on picking individual stocks. That's fine. You can build a portfolio that will be more than adequate, using a combination of ETFs. For example, you could construct ETFs that give exposure to:

- the ASX 200 companies
- the S&P 500
- emerging markets
- gold.

In this example, through four ETFs you can build a reasonably diversified portfolio that covers many companies, across many different countries, as well as some gold exposure. In only four ETFs! If you're just starting out, building up your core portfolio of ETFs might be an option worth considering

Core and satellite

There is an investment strategy known as 'core and satellite'. It refers to the way you construct a portfolio. It's where you build up a significant portion of your portfolio with passive ETF investments that track indexes. Then, once you've got that up and running, you can look to add some actively managed stocks—ones that might be more risky, but have the potential to generate some higher returns. These are known as your satellite stocks.

Do ETFs pay dividends?

Dividends, sometimes known as distributions, are the profits paid out by companies to their shareholders. It is not compulsory to pay dividends, and not all companies do. If a company does pay dividends, you receive a portion of the profit, depending on how many shares you own.

In general, if the companies that are in an ETF do pay dividends, then the ETF provider will pass on those dividends to you.

Some ETF providers also let you take part in distribution reinvestment plans (DRPs). This is where you can select to have some, or all, of your distributions reinvested back into the ETF, rather than paid to you in cash.

If you're young, and early in your investing journey, this is certainly worth considering. If you don't need the cash, it's worth considering reinvesting it back into the fund to increase your holding and then let compounding work its magic.

 LISTENER QUESTION
how do I know what's inside an ETF?

It's very important you look under the hood before you buy, to understand what companies are in the ETF. To do this, you need to go to the website of the ETF provider, whether it is in Australia or overseas.

Look for your ETF and then the 'holdings' section. It should look like something similar to the table below. (You should also be able to download it in an Excel file.) The table shows an example of the top ten holdings of the BetaShares A200 ETF. The weighting represents what percentage of the total portfolio that particular stock represents. For example, CSL makes up 7.9% of the total ETF.

PORTFOLIO HOLDINGS

Name	Weight (%)
CSL Ltd	7.9
Commonwealth Bank of Australia	7.4
BHP Group Ltd	6.2
National Australia Bank Ltd	4.1
Westpac Banking Group	3.8
Australia & New Zealand Banking Group	3.3
WesFarmers Ltd	3.0
Macquarie Group Ltd	2.8
Woolworths Group Ltd	2.7
Transurban Group	2.4

*As at 11 November 2020. Excludes cash.

ETF providers in Australia

There are six major providers of ETFs in the Australian market, all with a variety of different ETFs available on the ASX. The providers are:

- BetaShares ETFs
- ETF Securities
- iShares by BlackRock
- SPDR by State Street Global Advisors
- VanEck ETFs
- Vanguard Australia.

Still thinking 'WTF is an ETF?'

Don't stress—understanding how it all works can be challenging. The key thing to remember is that ETFs are a great way for you to start your investing journey, without feeling like you have to pick individual stocks.

They're a cost-effective way to get broad exposure to many markets around the world, and for you to back particular themes or industries you think will perform well in the future.

Start by having a look at the options available from the providers above, to understand what might work best for your situation. And remember: have fun with it!

 LISTENER QUESTION
what changes the price of an ETF?

Let's go back to our fruit salad analogy. The fruit salad is made up of bananas, apples, mangos, oranges and peaches. You buy it for $7. The price of the fruit salad is driven by the cumulative changes in price of each of the different types of fruit.

A simple, theoretical example: should the bananas go up in price by $5, the apples up by $6, but the mangoes drop by $3 and the oranges drop by $4, the price of the total fruit salad will go up $4. Why? $7 + $5 + $6 − $3 − $4 = $11.

This is a very basic example, but what it's showing is how the change in price of the underlying assets primarily drives the overall change in the price of the ETF. The price of an ETF that tracks the top 200 companies in Australia is driven by the cumulative change in all 200 companies during that day.

Back the professionals

Sometimes letting the professionals do the work for you can be a good option. If you don't want to choose ETFs or individual stocks, there is an alternative. It's called listed investment companies (LICs).

Sometimes the choice of what to buy can be too much, and you just want to let the professionals handle it. The great news is that you can do this through the stock market by buying **listed investment companies** (LICs).

 PARDON THE JARGON
listed investment company

A **listed investment company** is a company managed by a professional investor. Rather than the company making a product or offering a service, the company makes money by investing. It can be bought and sold on the stock market like any other public company.

There are many fund managers out there, running their own business and managing people's money. Some perform really well, others not so. They all try to specialise in different investing strategies, be it growth, Australian-only companies, small companies, emerging markets, you name it; there's a manager for everything.

Getting access to these managers is often difficult. It requires directly giving them your money, and usually the minimum amounts to invest are $10,000 or above. In some cases, it can be upwards of $250,000.

This is where LICs come into play. Some managers decide to list their funds on the ASX and make them available to retail investors like you and us. What this means is you can buy shares in their business, if you like the manager and their investing approach. They will actively manage their funds, based on their strategy.

The benefit is you can get exposure to some of the best managers, without having to fork out thousands for their private funds.

One thing to be conscious of is that, despite the performance of the manager and their fund, the stock price is still at the beck and call of the forces of supply and demand. If all of a sudden the fund manager falls out of favour with the market, and everyone sells the stock, it's likely the price will fall. This could be despite the fact their fund is performing okay.

On the flip side, if the market thinks the fund manager is a superstar, there will be demand for the stock, and it'll most likely rise. Unlike an ETF, the performance of the stock is not directly correlated to the underlying performance of the fund.

What to look for when investing in a listed investment company

Fees

Paying too much in fees can be the difference between getting rich and your investment manager getting rich. There is no 'right amount' of fees to pay. Sometimes you have to pay more for quality. There are two types of fees to look at:

- Management fee: taken from the amount you invested (e.g. if you invest $100, and the management fee is 2%, the fund will take $2 every year).
- Performance fee: taken from the profits the fund makes (e.g. if the firm makes $10 from your $100 investment, and charges a 20% performance fee, it will take 20% of the $10 profit, taking $2).

In this example, you invested $100 and made $10 profit. The fund took $4 in fees.

Investment strategy

There are plenty of ways to make money in the stock market, and you can find an LIC that follows any strategy you can think of. Do your research and make sure you're comfortable with the strategy being followed. Some common strategies include finding bargain stocks (value), finding fast-growing companies (growth) and finding companies that have a fast-growing share price (momentum).

Time horizon

Different LICs will have different time horizons. Some are set up to outperform over decades, others are more short term and set up to outperform every year (while outperformance every year sounds great, a shorter-term fund is likely to need to take more risks!). Make sure you're comfortable with the time horizon before investing (e.g. if you want to retire in a couple of years, a fund that invests for a decades-long time horizon isn't the right one for you).

What not to look at

One thing not to look too closely at: recent performance. Don't chase the LIC that has performed the best over the past couple of years. Just like everything in life, investing performance moves in cycles. In the same way that your favourite footy team will have a period where it competes for premierships before a period of rebuilding, an investment manager will outperform for a period of time and then have a period where they fall back to the pack.

Find a strategy you like, and stick with it.

What are some of my options?

There are too many to mention—there's plenty of choice out there, with different strategies and asset classes. Below are some links to give you an idea of what is out there. Then it is a matter of doing your research and finding LICs that work for you.

- ASX LICs: an up-to-date list of LICs trading on the Australian stock market. www.asxlics.com
- Morningstar Monthly LIC Report: offers a monthly look at how LICs have been performing. www.morningstar.com.au/LICs/MonthlyReports

How to find a company to invest in

If you've built your core portfolio of ETFs, or you're looking for something a bit more adventurous to test your skills, then it's time to think about investing in individual companies. The question is: how do you find one?

Finding opportunities to invest can often be the hardest part but there are plenty of resources available to help you.

As with anything, the more you practise looking for companies, and the more you become aware of opportunities, the easier your investing will become.

There is no magic formula (although we wish there were!), and it is entirely up to you to decide what to invest in. But it is incredibly fun and rewarding searching for that next great stock. Below are some resources available to you to help you find your next investment.

First a quick note: you won't get every stock pick right. That's fine. Some of the best investors in the world will admit they get three out of ten stock picks right. But those three are the ones that deliver huge returns.

Don't get too caught up on trying to pick the perfect one. Just get in there and have a go!

The world is your oyster

When you invest in individual stocks, there is so much to choose from. There are more than 2,000 companies listed in Australia, more than 4,000 in the USA and more than 40,000 around the world.

The opportunities seem endless.

The challenge is narrowing down the vast amount of stocks to a manageable size.

What are you looking for?

With so many great companies out there, the first thing to do is establish what you want to find. As you learn about some of these companies, what is it you're looking for?

At the end of the day, it's about companies that create a product or service that people want, can make a profit and use that profit to create more products or services that people want.

That's it.

It seems overly simplified, but basically everything in investing can be distilled down to that. Finding profitable companies that will be more profitable in the future. That's how companies become more valuable and their share prices go up.

 FROM THE EXPERTS
good genes for companies

In his book *Millennial Money*, **Patrick O'Shaughnessy** uses the analogy of genetics to explain what we should be looking for when trying to find great investments.

'Think about genetics for a moment. Some people are more prone to athletic excellence, others to heart disease. Stocks, just like people, have genes. Some stocks are more likely to outperform the market; others are more likely to underperform it. The best way to be different is to only own stocks with the best genes—the ones that are the most likely to

> outperform in the future. Good genes are things like cheap prices and
> strong earnings; bad genes are things like expensive prices and reckless
> corporate spending.'

The question becomes, how do you find companies with good genes?

Circle of competence

Knowing your circle of competence is one way to start looking for companies.

The concept of a circle of competence has been used by Warren Buffett to get investors to focus on finding businesses in areas they know and understand. Buffett is arguably the greatest investor in history, having amassed a fortune of more than US$86 billion by the age of 90.

In his 1996 Shareholder Letter he wrote: 'What an investor needs is the ability to correctly evaluate selected businesses. Note that word "selected": You don't have to be an expert on every company, or even many. You only have to be able to evaluate companies within your circle of competence. The size of that circle is not very important; knowing its boundaries, however, is vital.'

Through the experiences we have had in life, through our study, through our work, we have all built up areas of useful knowledge.

This knowledge, believe it or not, does help you to evaluate investment opportunities.

For example, you may work for a supermarket. You know what it takes to run the supermarket—staff, rent, buying and stocking inventory, marketing. You would likely know more than someone who didn't work in one, whereas you would probably struggle to know how a business that specialises in building rockets operates.

It's using this circle of competence to your advantage, and more importantly knowing what is *not* within your circle of competence. Trying to invest in stocks that you just don't understand can be a recipe for disaster.

INVEST IN WHAT YOU KNOW

Be aware of your circle, and take time to slowly grow it. As you do, avoid investing in areas you know nothing about.

Three ways you can narrow down your choices

Without needing to know a whole lot about analysing charts and company reports, there are three ways we believe you can identify investment opportunities.

1 Invest in what you know—use your experience

Pay attention to the companies that you're using in your own life. Have you stopped buying clothes in-store and started buying them online? Are there particular products your friends and family are recommending to you? Have you noticed certain brands being used more? All of this information is useful in determining what companies will succeed in the years ahead.

FROM THE EXPERTS
buy what you understand

Jack Trengove is a former professional AFL player. We asked him about his very first investment. His answer was a classic example of investing in what you know . . .

'Throughout my studies is when I first started taking more notice of the markets. The first company that I officially bought stock in was Catapult. The reason for that, and there is no more reason more to the fact that it's technology that athletes wear on their bodies that tracks GPS, and the data goes straight through to the fitness guys, and the coaches, and you can't hide anywhere, because it's tracking your every step. From my time within AFL footy, I just saw every AFL club had them and were using them every day of the week and I saw them across many different codes as well. There wasn't much of a thesis behind why I bought it, but more so because of the popularity and I thought it was going to keep growing.'

Another way is to consider what interests you. You may be interested in fashion, in sports, in cars or cooking and this is a great place to start. Think of products or brands that you like or that are selling well, and find out which companies produce them. Then put in some time to research the company and its competitors to help you form an opinion as to whether it's a good opportunity for investment.

You may also have experience in an industry. For example, you may work in retail and as such have a better understanding of trends, market conditions, customers' favourite brands or company performance. Use this to your advantage and as a starting point for your research.

For example, since Apple released the first iPhone in 2007, its share price is up nearly 2,000%. You didn't need to be an expert investor to realise iPhones were a game changer. You just needed to pay attention to what people were buying.

INVESTING OPPORTUNITIES
are all around you

2 Follow the leader

There are no points for originality in investing. Pay attention to what expert investors are writing and talking about, and put them on your list of stocks to watch.

There is plenty of information publicly available online detailing what professional investors are buying and selling. For example, many listed investment companies (LICs) will have a section of their website that shows what they currently have in their portfolio. If there is a particular manager or company that you think is performing well, it might be worth having a look at their holdings to get some inspiration.

Remember though, that the professionals don't always get it right. You do need to do some of your own research and develop your own opinions on why you want to invest in the stock. But paying attention to what expert investors are talking about and investing in is a great way to improve your investment opportunities.

3 Stock screeners and numbers

Companies make their key numbers available to the public. Look for companies that are growing their key metrics—revenue, profit, cash on hand—and add them to your watchlist. This is not an exhaustive list of key financial metrics, and it's worth having a look at a company's balance sheet to get an idea of more.

You can do this using stock screeners. Screeners allow you to research and filter companies based on specific parameters that are important to you. Just like when you're booking an Airbnb and you filter the search results to 'entire place', 'air conditioning', '<$200 per night', you can do the same for stocks.

If you want to find a company that is growing revenue at 15% or more a year, has no debt on its balance sheet and has positive cash flow, then a screener will give you a list of stocks that match these criteria.

There are many free screeners available online.

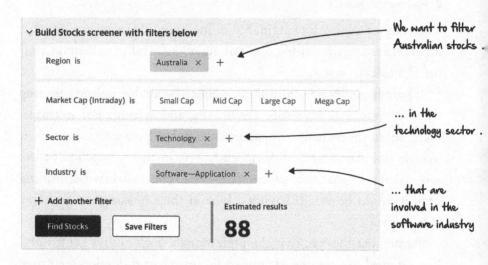

This is an example of a free stock screener available on Yahoo Finance. We were interested in narrowing down the Australian market to only companies in the technology sector that are providing software services. At the time of writing, the screener narrowed the list from more than 2,000 down to 88.

Key things to keep in mind when buying individual companies

We've covered a lot of ground. Let's just pause and recap the key points to be aware of when buying a company.

- Know what you are buying—don't blindly buy a stock because your friend told you it was a good idea. That's a recipe for disaster!
- Pay attention! Companies announce how they're performing. It's worth paying attention to this.
- Try not to spray and pray—a smaller portfolio with well-considered stocks might be a better option than one with many stocks that are wild guesses.
- Don't feel like you need to get it right each and every time. You will get some wrong.

How do the experts do it?

Getting insight into how the experts go about finding their next investment is incredibly useful. When they publicly share some of their process, it's certainly worth paying attention.

When Warren Buffett shares some of his process, you *must* pay attention. In a book called *Buffettology*, written by Warren's daughter, Mary Buffett, nine of Warren's key questions are shared. These questions form part of Warren's process of finding companies he could invest in.

Don't get too worried if you don't understand all of the terminology—the question and process is the important part.

As you progress with your journey, you can revert to this list as you understand more of what it's asking.

1 Is the business a monopoly?

This question is asking you to consider the strength of the company's brand. Does it have a strong brand that keeps customers coming back?

Is the brand so strong that its competitors find it hard to take market lead? Buffett asks himself 'how much damage could a competitor do if he didn't care about money?' Is the company's brand strong enough to withstand competitors throwing everything at them?

2 Does the company have strong earnings, and are they trending upward?

On the balance sheet you need to look for three letters: EPS—earnings per share. This is the measure used to analyse the earnings of the company. Once you've found EPS, look back over a number of years to see if it is in a strong, consistent upward trend. Remember, the key here is trend; not every year has to be higher than the previous one but over time the trend needs to be going up.

3 Does the company have a lot of debt?

Here we are looking at the level of debt the company has, and if it's good or bad debt. The general idea is that long-term debt shouldn't be much higher than current net earnings. Long-term debt you will find in the financial statements, and you will also find current net earnings there too. If the company has a lot of debt, have a look to try to understand why. Perhaps it purchased another company in the past year, which could be a good thing. If it appears the debt is from poor management, then perhaps it's best to reconsider.

4 Is there a consistent high rate of return on shareholders' equity?

Shareholders' equity is defined as a company's total assets minus the company's total liabilities (debt). It's like the equity in your house. If you bought an investment property for $200,000 and put in $50,000 of your own money and borrowed $150,000, the $50,000 is considered your equity. If you rented the house, after all expenses, the return you made from the rent is known as your return on equity. If you earned $5,000 after expenses from the rental income, then your earnings are

$5,000 from $50,000 invested. This means $5,000/$50,000 = 10% return on (shareholders') equity. If you invest in a company, just like you invest the $50,000, the earnings the company makes are split across all the shares and you get a return on your investment. Anything above a 12% return is above average.

5 Does the business retain its profits?

Does the business get to keep its earnings and use them to invest in growing the business, or does it have to pay out large sums of dividends to its shareholders? (Buffett generally likes businesses that reinvest their profits back into the business.) You can find this information in the financial statements. Just look for 'dividends' and 'retained earnings'.

6 How much does the business spend on keeping the lights on?

You don't want a business that has to spend an arm and a leg to keep afloat day to day. You want one that has to spend very little to keep running. The perfect business is one that makes $5 million and spends nothing on replacing its plant and equipment. You can find this information by looking for 'operating expenses' in the financial statements. If they are a large proportion compared to its earning and profits, then perhaps reconsider.

7 Is the management good at reinvesting money back into the business, for growth in the future?

This is similar to question 5. Can the company use its earnings to buy other companies or buy some of its own stock? Take note of the management; this is quite hard to do if you don't know what you're looking for, so to be honest, as long as there's not a lot of news about management getting fired or there aren't lots of changes on the board, then you can move onto the next one. It takes time to get used to 'reading' the management situation of businesses.

8 Can the company easily adjust its prices?

As inflation (the cost of goods and services) goes up, can the business change its prices or is it a commodity business where prices are set by the market? For example, Apple can decide to put up the price of their iPhone each year as the cost of living goes up. No one else makes iPhones, so it has the luxury to do that if they want. But a mining company can't just put up the price of the coal it sells, otherwise no one would buy from it. It's the laws of supply and demand. If the mining company overproduces, then it will have to lower the price of coal so it can get rid of excess supply.

9 Will investing back into the business result in the company being more valuable?

Here Buffett is asking if, by retaining earnings and investing back into the business, this will be reflected in the price of the stock. Obviously you hope the answer is yes, but it's not always the case. Buffett believes that if the answers to most of the questions above are yes, then over time the market will keep pushing up the price of the stock.

If this feels all way too complicated and advanced, don't worry. It took us a long time to get our heads around it too. These are concepts you will come to learn and build on as you go through you journey. For now, mark this page as one to come back to.

There's no one right way

We've demonstrated three ways you can narrow down the universe of stocks, and shown you how Buffett thinks about his options. The key thing to remember is that there is no one right way to finding your next big stock. Over time you might develop a process that works, but it will take time. Heck, Buffett is well past retirement age and he's still perfecting his craft!

Focus on the journey, and the discovery process, and learning from your mistakes. Keep your eyes and ears open, and pay attention to what's going on. You never know—the stock that could lead to your early retirement might be right under your nose!

Tips for buying and selling

When buying and selling shares, there are a few key considerations. We're going to unpack the ones that are important for your stage of the investing journey.

How do I know when is a good time to buy?

If there was a golden rule, then we'd all be billionaires. Knowing when is the right time to buy can be a paralysing thing to try to work out.

There are so many ways to determine when is a good time to buy, and it really comes down to your strategy.

Here are a few ways we think about it.

Don't try to time the market

You never know what the market is going to do. Trying to time it is a fool's game. One way to think about it is to look at the bigger picture. Rather than asking yourself 'Is today a good day to buy an ETF that tracks the ASX 200?', it might be better to think 'Are the next few months looking positive for the ASX 200?'

If your investment style is long term, and you're not looking for short-term gains, then the difference between entering at $55 in February or $58 in March or $52 in May is not worth stressing about over the long term.

Do the work before the trade

Understand what you're buying and what your thesis is. Having a thesis—a reason for buying a stock—is so important. If you can articulate the reasons you think this is a good investment, it will help with so many decisions going forward.

One tip is to write down your thesis. It can be 50 words, it can be 5,000 words! This really helps you to think about the pros and cons of the investment.

If you spend time understanding your company, or the industry, what drives its costs, where it generates its revenue, then you are going to be better equipped to know when to buy and sell than if you were taking a punt.

If you can determine that over the next five years an industry is likely to experience significant growth due to relaxed government regulation, for example, or significant advances in technology, then deciding what day to buy is less important. Remember: it's more about time in the market than timing the market.

How do I know when is a good time to sell?

To let compounding do its thing, and to take advantage of long-term market returns, the best thing to do is not to sell! Hold your winners for as long as you can. Let them run.

Sure, you're going to see a number of stocks in your portfolio lose money. That's inevitable. The key is to work out if it's because of market sentiment or because there is a fundamental change to the business. This is where your thesis helps.

Referring back to why you bought the company in the first place is perhaps the best way to know when to sell. If your thesis has changed, if the business has taken a different direction or the original reasons for buying the company are no longer applicable, then that is a good time to consider selling.

For example, if you bought a furniture company because it was able to manufacture furniture much more cheaply than its competitors with advanced technology, and it had an exclusive distribution agreement with Amazon, then you could argue it is in a position to beat its competitors for years to come.

But if a competitor comes along with better technology or Amazon opens up distribution to other furniture manufacturers, then your original thesis has changed. Your furniture company might not be able to compete with the new competitor and as a result its revenue might fall. This is a good opportunity to consider selling.

Otherwise, if there has been no change to your thesis, you need to ask yourself, 'why would I sell?'

Other reasons you might want to sell:

- You have reached your investing goal, and want to sell to use the cash to buy a home or go on a holiday.
- You want to cash out some profits, and rebalance your portfolio into other stocks.
- You want to cut your losses and move on to another investment opportunity.
- The price other investors are willing to pay for your shares is so high compared to what you think your shares are worth.

The market's up, the market's down—what should I do?

The stock market is constantly changing; every day it is up or down. There are times when the stock market is down a lot (e.g. in March 2020, at the start of the Covid-19 pandemic, the market lost a third of its value in a month) and there are times when the market is up a lot (e.g. American technology stocks almost tripled in value between 2018 and 2020).

You might be reading *Get Started Investing* in a tough period for the stock market, or an incredibly good period. Should you buy now, should you wait for a better moment?

Start googling this question and you'll get plenty of conflicting answers. Everyone has an opinion and you'll end up more confused than when you started.

Forget all that noise, here's what we've learnt over our journey.

- The #1 rule is: time in the market beats timing the market. Which simply means—over time the market trends up and historically it has been better to buy regardless of whether the market is up or down.
- Market falls offer great buying opportunities. When the stock market is cheap, and other investors are fearful, you can invest at a great price.
- Once the market has fallen, don't sell. Most of the time all you'll do is miss the recovery and lock in your loss. Close your computer, put your phone away and stop watching the daily market movements. Over time the stock market will recover.
- Never invest any money you'll need for your day-to-day living expenses. Always have an emergency fund in cash that you do not invest in the stock market. That'll allow you to invest without needing to sell your investments to cover expenses in an emergency.

Section summary
YOUR PROGRESS

☑ WHY INVEST
☑ BUILD AN INVESTOR MINDSET
☑ GET YOUR MONEY RIGHT
☑ UNDERSTANDING THE BASICS

☑ TAKING THE PLUNGE

You're now ready to take the plunge and start your investing journey. Between micro-investing, ETFs, listed investment companies and individual shares, there's so much opportunity in the investing world. Focus on investing for the long term: you care about how your money will grow in three to five years, not three to five minutes.

The same goes for the information you're reading. There's so much online that it can be overwhelming. Ignore the day-to-day media cycle and focus on the bigger picture. When thinking about what to invest, there's information everywhere. Narrow your search down by thinking about what you're using and what the experts are doing, and by using the free online tools like stock screeners.

You have:
✓ signed up to a micro-investing app to start small
✓ grown in confidence and chosen a broker who's good enough to start your journey for now
✓ found a few good sources of information that focus on the big-picture stuff
✓ bought your first ETF!
✓ perhaps even bought your first stock! Well done!

☐ BEYOND THE FIRST INVESTMENT
☐ LESSONS WE WISH WE HAD KNOWN
☐ PULLING IT ALL TOGETHER

PART 7

Beyond the First Investment

Once you start you can't stop!

Building a portfolio

You've taken the plunge and made your first investment: maybe it was an ETF, a managed fund or an individual stock. Whatever it was, we hope it won't be your last. Now's the time to turn that first investment into a portfolio.

Having an investment portfolio—now you're getting deep into finance. Soon you'll have a sleeveless Patagonia vest and promote your Excel skills on your Tinder profile.

The term **portfolio** is used a lot by investors. There's nothing too complicated to it; it's really just the term for the collection of your investments.

PARDON THE JARGON
investment portfolio

A **portfolio** is a collection of investments held by a person or an organisation. It is not just limited to stocks, but can include any investments—everything from property to art or whatever else you consider an investment.

Remember: diversification

We introduced the concept of diversification in Part 5. A portfolio is where it becomes very important. When you're building your portfolio you want to ensure you've spread your money across multiple investments so you're not overly exposed to one form of risk.

You don't want one bad event to blow up everything you've worked so hard to build. You wouldn't put all your investments in different coal companies because there is a risk that renewable energy technology will dramatically hurt the coal mining industry. Similarly, don't have all Australian investments, so a recession in Australia doesn't send everything down.

Whatever the portfolio you build, keep it diversified.

Types of portfolios

There are plenty of different 'types' of portfolios. The type of portfolio that is right for you depends on your tolerance for risk and your investing goals.

Your portfolio setting will change over time. Much like superannuation, you generally start more aggressively when you're younger and then get safer and more defensive as you get older.

Here are a few different types that give you a sense of what is out there.

- An income-focused portfolio: focused on investments that pay the investor income, rather than investments that grow in value. This is focused on bonds, real estate and dividend-paying stocks.
- A defensive portfolio: this is focused on slow-growing, blue-chip companies that aren't expected to grow quickly but also won't lose your money. This portfolio should do okay in bad economic times, protecting your hard-earned investments.
- A balanced hybrid portfolio: this takes a 'little bit of everything' approach. Some defensive assets, some income-paying assets, then some that are a little more risky but expected to grow faster.
- An aggressive equities portfolio: as you get aggressive, you are taking more risk with your money. You are looking for smaller companies that are maybe not household names yet and that have a lot of room

to grow. If things go well, these investments could make you a lot of money. If they don't, they could lose you a lot.

- A speculative equities portfolio: this is the highest risk, highest reward setting. You're focused on companies in the early stages of growth. These are companies that no one has ever heard of, and could either go spectacularly right or spectacularly wrong.

Portfolio construction

Once you've decided on the type of portfolio that makes sense for you, you can start planning what you're actually going to buy. This introduces the concepts of **asset allocation** and **portfolio weighting**.

PARDON THE JARGON
asset allocation and portfolio weighting

Asset allocation is investing jargon for 'what are you going to buy'. It refers to the mix of different investments that will make up your portfolio.

If asset allocation is about 'what you will buy', then **portfolio weighting** is asking 'how much you will buy'. Weighting is usually expressed as a percentage, so you might hear an investor say 'I have a 30% weighting towards bonds'. This just means they've invested 30% of their money in bonds.

This doesn't need to be a complicated process, but does deserve some thought. While there are some general rules around portfolio weighting and asset allocation that we've learnt from the experts we've spoken to, it is an individual decision affected by your individual financial circumstances and goals.

This is where a financial adviser can really come in handy. To read more about financial advisers and to find one near you, head to the Australian Government's Money Smart website.

building a portfolio

We spoke to a couple of experts about the rules they follow when building a portfolio.

Andy Hart is the founder of UK-based Maven Adviser. He spoke to us about the importance of diversification in his portfolio.

'Diversification is a financial superpower—so massively underrated. It falls into the camp of a free lunch. So globally, well-diversified equity portfolios are where all your returns are going to come from. And it's, as I say, a financial superpower to understand diversification.'

Ted Richards is the Director of Business Development at Six Park and a former premiership-winning AFL player. He spoke to us about the importance of asset allocation in his portfolio.

'It can make sense to structure your portfolio to achieve returns on your asset allocation rather than focusing purely on individual stock selection. Also, many people worry far too much about how to time the market with their contributions, and they end up sitting on cash for far too long. Short-term market gyrations are impossible to predict, so just regularly add to your portfolio and if required re-balance your asset allocation if it has drifted.'

Building a portfolio through the stock market

Once you have decided what assets are going to make up your portfolio, the good news is you can access the majority of them through the stock market.

Here are a few of the major asset classes and a few ways you can access them on the stock market. This list is by no means exhaustive, so jump online and do your own research to decide what would work for you.

Asset class	How you can access it
Stocks	As well as buying individual stocks, you can buy ETFs or managed funds that invest in individual stocks
Property	Forget the idea that you need to take a mortgage out to own property. There are REITs (real estate investment trusts) and ETFs that own property and you can buy these on the stock market.
Bonds	You don't need to lend money to governments or companies to own a bond. You can buy ETFs that hold bonds of some of the major governments and companies around the world.
Gold and other commodities	There are funds and ETFs that hold every commodity you can think of. The major ones—gold, silver, natural gas, oil, sugar—and plenty you wouldn't think to invest in—pork belly, diamonds, corn, soybeans.

Overwhelmed by the options?

There are so many options available on the stock market it can be difficult to know what to buy. Even once you know what you want to buy, it can be difficult to know how much you should own. It is one of the most common questions in the Equity Mates community.

 LISTENER QUESTION

how much of your portfolio should be made up of individual stocks and other assets?

This is a difficult question to answer, because it depends on your personal financial circumstances and risk tolerance. The first piece of advice is to speak to a licensed financial adviser. They can help take into account all of your personal circumstances and build a bespoke portfolio suited to you.

Over the journey we've come across a number of pieces of general advice or rules of thumb that can help you think about your personal answer to this question.

- **Sliding scale:** when you're younger, you can afford to take more risk in your investments. As you get older, and get closer to retirement, you should take less risk and protect your investments. One rule of thumb we've come across is to subtract your age from 110. That is the percentage that should be allocated to stocks. For example, if you're 40, then 110 − 40 is 70, so 70% of your money should be allocated to stocks.
- **Have clear goals:** understanding what you're trying to achieve with your investments is critical to building your portfolio. If you want to generate income, property and bonds may be your best option. If you want aggressive growth, stocks may be the choice. If you want to protect your money, cash or gold may be the play. At the end of the day, it'll be a mix of all of the above. The exact mix will depend on your goals.
- **Diversify, diversify, diversify:** we've said it before and we'll say it again. Diversification is key. Whatever your mix of investments, make sure they are not exposed to the same source of risk. There's no point owning gold, shares in goldmining companies and bonds of those same goldminers. If something goes wrong with the price of gold, they'll all lose value.
- **Have at least 5% cash:** cash isn't a good investment, but it does give you options. Having some cash on hand lets you take advantage of a market fall. A number of financial advisers suggest 5% of your money in cash, but again, it comes down to your personal circumstances and preferences.

Four pillars supporting your portfolio

There's a lot of investing advice out there. So much conflicting advice, so much noise. It can get confusing. The amount of investing-related content being pumped out online is staggering. Whatever opinion you can think of, there's probably a podcast, YouTube channel, Twitter account or investing blog that shares that opinion.

We've sifted through a lot of it over the past few years as we went on our own investing journeys. Here we've condensed some of the lessons that we thought were most important.

These are the general pieces of advice or questions that we've asked ourselves that have helped in building our investing portfolios. More importantly, they are a lot of the lessons we've learnt from the experts we've interviewed on the podcast.

We've found that it helps to think about four key 'pillars' when building your portfolio: goals, risk, diversification and asset allocation.

1 Investing goals and your portfolio

Back in Part 2 we covered off investing goals—finding the 'why' for your investing.

This goal is particularly relevant when building a portfolio because it will determine the type of assets you invest in.

- If your goal was to build an income stream to eventually replace your salary, then you need to have an income component to your portfolio.
- If your goal was to retire as soon as possible, then you need to aggressively pursue growth.
- If you want to build intergenerational wealth and pass on a nest egg to your kids, then the focus can be more defensive and slower growing investments.

2 Risk

Once you've set your investing goals, the next step is to think about your risk appetite. It's all good and well to set the goal to be a millionaire by 30, but if you are not able to stomach the risk that such a strategy entails, then you need to temper your goals.

It's important to remember that the riskier your strategy is, the more likely you are to lose your money.

A lot of new investors decide that they are willing to take on a very risky strategy, but the first time they see themselves lose a lot of money, they realise they maybe weren't up for that level of risk.

3 Diversification

The amount we're speaking about diversification, we're starting to sound like a broken record. But it is important and a key pillar of any portfolio.

We won't repeat what we've already said about diversification. Just keep it in mind.

4 Asset allocation

The final pillar of portfolio construction is asset allocation. This is about the amount of money you invest in different assets.

The reason this is important is that different assets perform differently. They have different characteristics and act in different ways.

For example, if an investor wants to get paid an income every year, they should be allocating more of their assets (putting more of their money) towards stocks that pay dividends or property they can rent. If an investor is more focused on protecting their money and less worried about growth, then gold or bonds should get a bigger percentage of their investments. Then, if an investor wants to see more growth, stocks should have a larger percentage.

Your asset allocation will likely change over your life. For most people, when they're young, asset allocation is focused on growth and as they get closer to retirement, income and protecting your money becomes more important.

Unsure about these four pillars?

This is where a financial adviser can help. Head to ASIC's Money Smart website and find a government-licensed financial adviser near you.

Forget the buzzwords: what does it all mean?

At the end of the day, portfolio construction can be a complicated explanation for a few simple concepts. Invest in assets that make sense for you (i.e. if you want income every year, invest in assets that pay income) and don't put all your eggs in one basket.

Don't go all in on one country (i.e. Australia), one asset class (i.e. property) or one theme (i.e. software companies).

Adding more money to your investments

At this point you know your strategy for building your investment portfolio. Now the question is how you actually do it. In this section we get into the nuts and bolts of actually building your portfolio.

After the excitement of your first investment dies down, the journey of lifelong investing really begins. Getting your saving habits set, putting money away and then regularly putting it into the market.

The question becomes: how do I do it? Should I be investing every week, every month, every year? Should I be buying new stocks every time?

In this section we cover some of the key questions we had to answer as we went on our investing journeys. Perhaps the biggest one is this: when is the right time to invest?

Don't worry about timing the market

Every day, stock prices move up and down. You can lose a lot of sleep and create a lot of stress trying to pick the perfect time to buy a stock. The good news is that all that stress is unnecessary. You can sleep easy. Over the long term, the stock market recovers and slowly and consistently grinds upwards.

If you zoom out and look at the American stock market with a long time horizon, you can see that the chaotic market crashes look like small interruptions to the overall growth we've seen.

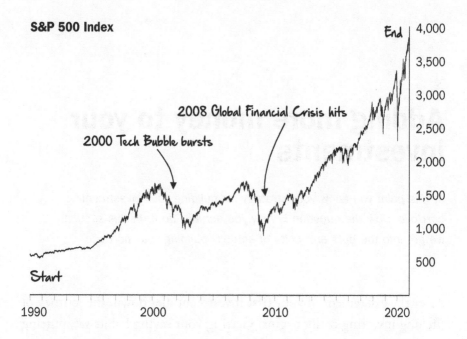

S&P 500 Index

Start

2000 Tech Bubble bursts

2008 Global Financial Crisis hits

End

Our favourite example of this is during the 2008 Global Financial Crisis. The first bank to collapse during the financial crisis was Lehman Brothers. Lehman collapsed on a Monday (Monday, 15 September 2008 to be specific). Let's assume you bought an index fund tracking America's S&P 500 on the Friday before the Monday collapse of Lehman Brothers:

- Six months later, in early March, you would have lost almost half your money (down 46% on 6 March 2009).
- Ten years later, you would have more than doubled your money (up 132% on 12 September 2018).

Sure, you would have made more money if you'd bought right at the bottom. The problem is: how do you know when the market has hit the bottom? We're going to answer our own question here: you don't. Often when you try to pick the bottom of the market, you miss out as the market starts to recover.

We spoke to Equity Mates community member, Alf, and he left us with a quote that has always stayed with us:

'The thing is, you can try to pick the bottom, but if you try to pick the bottom, you end up with a stinky finger.'

History has shown that even buying at the absolute worst times isn't worth stressing about. If you're focusing on the long term, you'll be okay.

If we go back to the 2008 Global Financial Crisis, if you had spread out when you invested, you would have invested some when the market was higher (which turned out okay) and some when the market was lower (which would have turned out even better).

By just automatically investing a bit every month, you would have saved yourself the stress of trying to perfectly time when to buy and also captured some of the benefit of buying when the market fell.

Forget the idea of 'buying low'. Replace it with 'buy regularly'.

This brings us back to the concept of dollar-cost averaging (which we introduced in Part 6).

Dollar-cost averaging, at the end of the day, is all about not saving your money and trying to pick the perfect time. Instead it focuses on investing regularly and consistently.

Forget saving up $5,000 to invest. Put that money to work in the market in 5 × $1,000 chunks as you save.

When you dollar-cost average, you sometimes buy when the share price is high and you sometimes buy when the share price is low. Over time, these average out.

By doing this, you can forget the worry about 'buying at the wrong time' and just buy regularly instead.

Example of dollar-cost averaging—Cleanaway and Coles

Have a look at these two charts of share prices: one is of Australia's largest waste company, Cleanaway, and the other is of Australia's second-largest supermarket chain, Coles. Since the start of 2020, their share prices have gone up and down, influenced by everything from Covid-19 concerns to changes in government policy. It would cause a serious amount of confusion if you were trying to find the perfect time to buy.

Don't.

Dollar-cost average instead.

Cleanaway

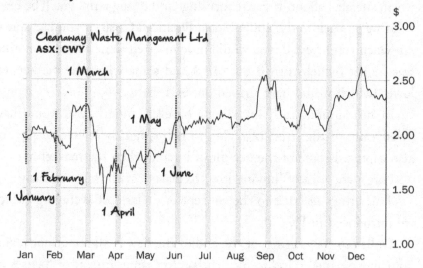

Here's the comparison of how you would have gone.

- If you'd bought Cleanaway on the first day of the year, you would be up 11% on your investment.
- If you had dollar-cost averaged and bought on the first of every month for six months, you'd be up 14% on your investment. You would have actually lost money on the stock you bought in March (down 3%). On the flip side, you would have done particularly well on the stock you bought in April and May (up 24% and 25% respectively).

You can see how, over time, the highs and lows of the share price smooth out.

Coles

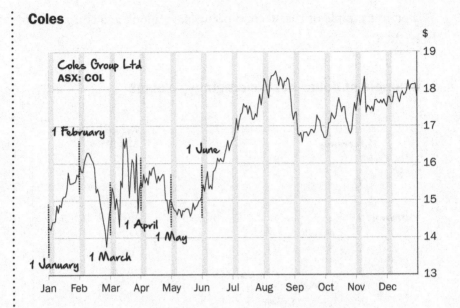

Coles Group Ltd
ASX: COL

Here's a second comparison of dollar-cost averaging in action.

- If you'd bought Coles shares at the start of the year, you would be up 23% on your investment.
- If you had dollar-cost averaged and bought stock on the first day of the month for six months, you'd be up 19%. February would have been your worst month (up 12%) and March would have been your best month (up 25%) but over time these highs and lows average out.

As you can see in these two examples, dollar-cost averaging isn't about making more money. Sometimes you do (like in our Cleanaway example) and sometimes you don't (like in our Coles example).

Dollar-cost averaging does two things:

1 It takes the stress out of deciding 'when to buy' by automating the process.
2 It protects you from buying at the absolute worst time.

For an example of that second point, have a look at a third example from 2020.

Example of dollar-cost averaging—Webjet

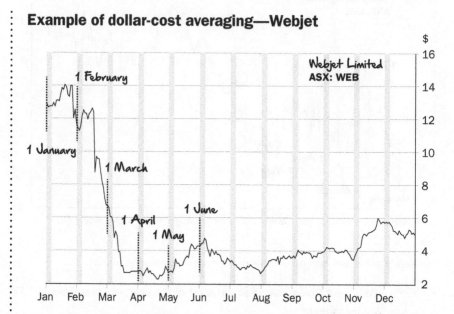

This chart shows the impact Covid-19 has had on the travel industry. At one stage, Webjet had lost three-quarters of its value as Covid lockdowns kept everyone grounded.

- If you had bought Webjet on the first day of the year, you would be down 56% on your investment. Ouch.
- If you had dollar-cost averaged and bought on the first of every month for six months, you'd still be down, but only down 8%. The stock you bought pre-Covid would be down significantly (down 56% in January and down 50% in February) but the stock you bought at the depths of Covid would actually be up (up 51% in April and up 47% in May).

This was dollar-cost averaging smoothing out the highs and lows and protecting you from buying at the very worst time.

LISTENER QUESTION
how often should I invest if I'm dollar-cost averaging?

There is no optimal time to dollar-cost average. The main thing is that you decide a frequency and dollar amount that you can commit to, so you keep it consistent.

The majority of people get paid either fortnightly or monthly, so a lot of people find it easier to sync up their investing with their pay cycle. That might be the best way to get started.

Some of the most common questions

Aside from 'when should I invest' there are a few other key questions that are worth discussing. Here are two more common questions the Equity Mates community have when it comes to building their portfolio.

LISTENER QUESTION
how much do I invest?

It would be great if there was a simple answer to this question. A magic number—$1,000 a month—or a magic ratio—10% of your monthly income. Unfortunately, like so many things in investing, it depends on your personal circumstances. There isn't a simple, universal answer.

But our general answer to this question is 'as much as possible'. You should only invest money that you are prepared to lose. Definitely nothing that you need to cover bills or monthly expenses. Start there—make sure you pay everything you need to pay.

The next step is to ensure you've got savings to cover any of life's emergencies. Opinions of personal finance experts differ on how big your emergency fund should be, but the Australian Government's Money Smart website suggests it should be enough to cover three months of expenses. Make sure you've got your emergency fund sorted. Just in case.

Once you've got that sorted, remember that you're investing for the long term. Don't invest money that you're planning to spend on a house down payment or an overseas holiday. The worst thing that could happen is that you are ready to head off on your holiday, you go to sell your stocks, and you have lost money. Keep that money saved.

Anything that is left over can be invested. For a lot of people, that may not be a lot. For some people, there may not be anything left over. That's okay. Starting small is better than not starting at all. Use a micro-investing app, focus on getting into good saving habits, kill it at your job and work for that raise, and—when you get that raise—don't let your lifestyle get more expensive. Live frugally now; your future self will thank you.

 LISTENER QUESTION
should I buy new stocks every time or invest more in stocks I already own?

Hope you're not sick of this answer already, because we're going to give it again. It depends.

If you are dollar-cost averaging, you should continue averaging into the same stocks, funds or ETFs. If this is not what you are doing or if you have some extra money to invest, there is no simple answer.

When it comes to investing, we're a big fan of the saying 'don't let perfection be the enemy of the good' and it really applies here. The main thing is that you're investing this money.

That being said, here's a few factors to consider when deciding if you want to invest in something new or double down on what you already own.

- Diversification: How much of this investment do you already own? Is it a large percentage of your portfolio? If so, make sure you're diversifying to reduce the risk in your portfolio.
- Is it actually different? A lot of different funds and ETFs may actually invest in very similar stocks. If you own an ETF that holds large technology stocks you don't need to invest in Apple or Microsoft as individual stocks. You already have those stocks in your portfolio through the ETF.
- If you've found a winner, why look elsewhere? If you've found a stock that you think you think is first class, don't invest in a second-class company just for the sake of it.

Patience and holding winners

We began Get Started Investing *talking about the long-term
benefits of compounding, how investing is this great pursuit where
doing nothing is often the best thing to do. Well this is where it
really comes into play. Once you have a portfolio and have set
rules about how you add to it, all there is to do is wait.*

Patience is hard. If a stock you hold is down, you often want to sell
and buy something new. If a stock is up, you often want to sell and
take the profits.

Resists these urges. Being a long-term investor often means doing
absolutely nothing.

History shows that even some of the best-performing stocks have
periods of underperformance. These weeks or months or sometimes
even years of poor performance would make you think you should
sell. But as the examples in the illustrations—Northern Star Resources,
Domino's Pizza and Games Workshop—show, that's the opposite of
what you should do.

All three of these stocks had months of underperformance followed
by very strong price increases. You'd be kicking yourself if you sold and
then watched some other investor get those returns.

Investing is not linear. Things don't go straight up. Stock prices
bounce up and down; sometimes they stay flat for a while. It's the long
term you want to focus on.

Some great stocks and their worst periods

AUSTRALIA—NORTHERN STAR RESOURCES

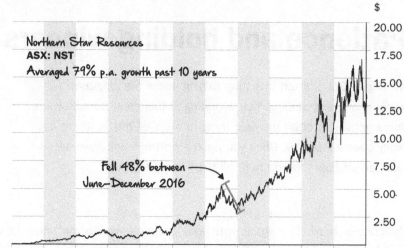

Northern Star Resources
ASX: NST
Averaged 79% p.a. growth past 10 years

Fell 48% between June–December 2016

USA—DOMINO'S PIZZA

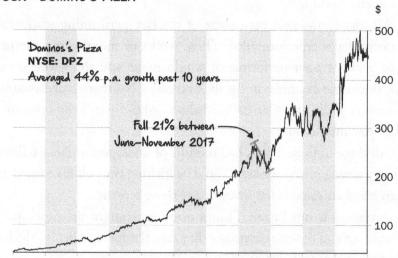

Dominos's Pizza
NYSE: DPZ
Averaged 44% p.a. growth past 10 years

Fell 21% between June–November 2017

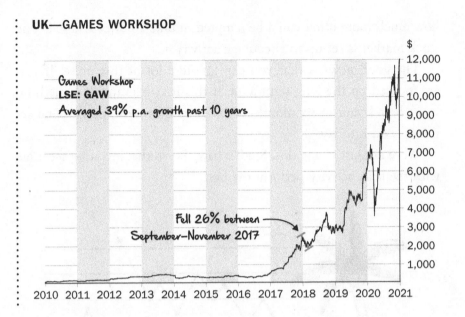

UK—GAMES WORKSHOP

Games Workshop
LSE: GAW
Averaged 39% p.a. growth past 10 years

Fell 26% between
September–November 2017

The less activity, the better

A lot of people in the finance industry have an incentive to encourage activity. The more activity, the more money they make. Stockbrokers make money when clients buy and sell, so they want you to be active. Financial media firms make money from the views, clicks and downloads of their reporting, so they want you looking at the stock market every day.

The market itself is set up for constant activity. The market is open every working day and is updating prices every second it is open.

Imagine if other investments worked this way. When you buy a house, you don't get someone knocking on your door every day telling you what you could sell the house for. Imagine if they did. Imagine how much more often you'd be tempted to take an offer and sell. The stock market is set up to encourage activity.

The good news is that you can ignore a lot of this noise. If you are focused on the long term a lot of this isn't relevant. If something won't be relevant in six months or six years from now, don't spend six minutes on it today.

We're not just saying this. Studies have shown that investing accounts with the least activity perform the best.

INVEST, RELAX, WAIT.

The secrets of the best-performing accounts

STUDY 1: FIDELITY'S BEST-PERFORMING ACCOUNTS

There is a story, so often repeated that it has become investing folklore, about US broker Fidelity's review of their best-performing investment accounts.

They looked at the best-performing accounts from 2003 to 2013 and noticed something strange.

The best-performing accounts were owned by dead people or people who had forgotten they had an account. These accounts hadn't been closed and were just left to sit there for ten years. No activity, no buying or selling, just holding.

Fidelity are not able to confirm that this study took place, so this may just be investing folklore. The good news is that there are plenty of actual studies that come to similar conclusions.

STUDY 2: UC BERKELEY STUDY OF RETAIL INVESTORS

A study that did happen, Professor Brad Barber and Professor Terry Odean's look at 66,000 retail investors in the 1990s, found that the highest traders had the worst results, whereas those who barely touched their accounts enjoyed the best results.

A side note to this study by two Berkeley professors was that women performed better than men. The average woman outperformed the average man by 1% per year. The reason? Women in the study traded 45% less often than the men.

As the study title suggested, 'trading is hazardous to your wealth'. The study showed the problem of being overly active in the stock market. So do yourself a favour, and be lazy.

 FROM THE EXPERTS
the danger of activity

Benjamin Graham was a British-born American economist and writer of some of the most famous investing books. He is widely known as the 'father of value investing'.

> 'The investor's chief problem—and even his worst enemy—is likely to be himself.'

John Maynard Keynes was a British economist who revolutionised the practice of macroeconomics and government economic policy.

> 'Investment is intolerably boring and overexacting to anyone who is entirely exempt from the gambling instinct; whilst he who has it must pay to this propensity the appropriate toll.'

If long-term investing is the best, why doesn't everyone do it?

The obvious question that comes from this is: if long-term, buy-and-hold investing is the best approach to investing, why isn't everyone doing it?

There are two key reasons that this is the case: one is behavioural and the other stems from the structure of the investment industry.

The behavioural reason we've touched on above. As humans, we're impatient. We want to get rich quick and so are always looking for the next big thing. The culture of sharing stock tips at barbecues, in WhatsApp groups and, these days, over TikTok videos is driven by this desire to get a 'quick win'.

Forget that. The 'slow wins' are a lot bigger.

The second reason has to do with the incentive structures for professional investors. Buying and holding great businesses for decades may be the best way to build long-term wealth, but it isn't the best way to keep your short-term employment.

Professional money managers are judged quarterly and have to show a good return every quarter. If they don't, the people whose money they're managing might go to another manager or their employer might decide they aren't performing. There are promotions and bonuses on the line. Professional investors don't have the time that we do as everyday people. They are incentivised to think more short term.

FROM THE EXPERTS

why fund managers have a short-term view

Seth Klarman is an American billionaire investor and author of the investing book *Margin of Safety*.

'Like dogs chasing their own tails, most institutional investors have become locked into a short-term, relative-performance derby. Fund managers at one institution have suffered the distraction of hourly performance calculations; numerous managers are provided daily comparisons of their results with those of managers at other firms. Frequent comparative ranking can only reinforce a short-term investment perspective. It is understandably difficult to maintain a long-term view when, faced with the penalties for poor short-term performance, the long-term view may well be from the unemployment line.'

Patrick O'Shaughnessy is the CEO of O'Shaughnessy Asset Management and author of *Millennial Money*.

'To minimise their "career risk", professionals make decisions that sacrifice large potential long-term rewards in favour of more secure short-term returns, or at least returns that are similar to the overall market.'

The opportunity for long-term thinkers

The fact that many professional money managers are incentivised to think more short term creates a big opportunity. This opportunity is labelled 'time horizon **arbitrage**', which is a complex term for a simple concept.

 PARDON THE JARGON
arbitrage

Arbitrage is most broadly defined as when investors take advantage of mispricing in a market.

The classic example of arbitrage is when an asset is traded in two markets at different prices. An investor buys the asset in the market where it is cheaper and sells the asset in the market where it is more expensive, pocketing the difference.

Think about someone who sees a car for sale on Gumtree for $5,000 but knows that same car sells on CarSales.com for $7,000. The investor buying the car on Gumtree and then turning around and selling it on CarSales is an example of arbitrage.

When we talk about 'time horizon arbitrage' we mean that we take advantage of stocks being mispriced based on their long-term potential.

If a company is having some short-term struggles, professional investors who are looking for a short-term return may underprice this asset. A company doesn't even need to be struggling: if a company has a three- to five-year strategy, many investors may not have the time to wait for a strategy to play out, so they undervalue the future prospects of the company.

This is where we, as everyday investors who don't have to report our results quarterly or annually, can swoop in. We can buy these great businesses and hold them for decades. There are no repercussions if the stock price doesn't move for three years. We don't have a boss looking over our shoulder asking us what's going on. We aren't missing out on annual bonuses because we didn't hit our numbers.

Our ability to be patient is our edge over the professionals. Use it.

FROM THE EXPERTS
the importance of a long time horizon

These are our favourite quotes from professional investors that explain the value of having a long-term view.

> 'The inability of so many investors and managers to invest with a long-term horizon creates the opportunity for time arbitrage—an edge in an investing approach that requires the commitment to long-term holding periods.'
> **JOEL GREENBLATT**

> 'The single greatest edge an investor can have is a long-term orientation.'
> **SETH KLARMAN**

> 'I think one of the inefficiencies in the market is investors are generically too short-term oriented and time arbitrage is one of the best inefficiencies in the market.'
> **DAVID EINHORN**

> 'If you invest the way people gamble at casinos you're not going to do very well. It's the long-term investment that works best. But if you like the

action of investing, sometimes winning, sometimes losing, just like the action in the casino, those people are not my people. I like the long-term investors who figure out something that is going to work over the long term and buy that.'

CHARLIE MUNGER

'Time arbitrage just means exploiting the fact that most investors—institutional, mutual funds or hedge funds—tend to have very short-term horizons, have rapid turnover or are trying to exploit very short-term anomalies. So the market looks extremely efficient in the short run. In an environment with massive short-term data overload and with people concerned about minute-to-minute performance, the inefficiencies are likely to be looking out beyond, say, twelve months.'

BILL MILLER

'It is just appalling the nerve strain people put themselves under trying to buy something today and sell it tomorrow. It's a small-win proposition. If you are a truly long-range investor, of which I am practically a vanishing breed, the profits are so tremendously greater.'

PHIL FISHER

'Over the last few decades, investors' timeframes have shrunk. They've become obsessed with quarterly returns. In fact, technology now enables them to become distracted by returns on a daily basis, and even minute-by-minute. Thus one way to gain an advantage is by ignoring the "noise" created by the manic swings of others and focusing on the things that matter in the long term.'

HOWARD MARKS

'Instead of focusing on the next quarter, investors need to focus on the next decade.'

STEPHEN PAICE

'We rely on concentrated research to identify great businesses that are trading at highly discounted valuations because investors have overreacted to negative macro or company specific events. That's the time arbitrage part of the strategy, taking advantage when the market reacts to short-term factors that have little impact on long-term intrinsic values.'

BILL ACKMAN

'The longer you can extend your time horizon the less competitive the game becomes, because most of the world is engaged over a very short time frame.'

WILLIAM BROWNE

'The advantage we have is time frame. When I came into the business the average holding period for a mutual fund was seven years. Today it's less than nine months.'

ROB RODRIGUEZ

How do you actually find long-term companies?

We could write a whole book on this (and many people have) but here are a few key lessons we've picked up on our own investing journeys.

- **Industry leaders:** find the best companies in each industry. The companies that create better products and services, that customers love and that have developed strong brands and customer loyalty are likely to keep winning. Companies like Nike, Walmart, Disney, Bunnings, Qantas and Woolworths are industry leaders because they are loved by their customers.

- **Best people:** people often make the difference. Companies like Apple and Amazon have been able to dominate their industries and become great long-term investments because they were led by brilliant CEOs (Steve Jobs and Jeff Bezos) and were constantly working to hire the most talented employees. The people they hired then allowed them to continue innovating and creating new products and services.

- **Disruptive industry:** industries that are being disrupted by new technology or new ways to do business often lead to long-term winners. Think about how PayPal disrupted the online payments market or Uber disrupted the taxi industry. These companies became massive and made their investors a lot of money because they found a better way to offer products and services to their customers.

Don't swing at every pitch

If you're going to be long term, you've got to be discerning. There are thousands of good companies out there. The best investors don't settle for good. They are only looking for great.

WARREN BUFFETT
the 20-slot rule

Legendary investor **Warren Buffett** has a '20-slot' rule that he teaches when discussing investing. His investing partner (and legendary investor in his own right) **Charlie Munger** explained it when lecturing at USC Business School:

'When Warren lectures at business schools, he says, "I could improve your ultimate financial welfare by giving you a ticket with only 20 slots in it so that you had 20 punches—representing all the investments that you got to make in a lifetime. And once you'd punched through the card, you couldn't make any more investments at all."

He says, "Under those rules, you'd really think carefully about what you did and you'd be forced to load up on what you'd really thought about. So you'd do so much better."

Again, this is a concept that seems perfectly obvious to me. And to Warren it seems perfectly obvious. But this is one of the very few business classes in the U.S. where anybody will be saying so. It just isn't the conventional wisdom.

To me, it's obvious that the winner has to bet very selectively. It's been obvious to me since very early in life. I don't know why it's not obvious to very many other people.'

Warren Buffett's 20-slot rule is worth thinking about, but is a really difficult concept to put into practice. Investing in only twenty companies over a lifetime is near impossible. In fact, Buffett and Munger have often been invested in more than twenty companies at one time . . .

But the underlying lesson is a good one. You need to be willing to let plenty of opportunities go by. There will always be more opportunities than you have money to invest. Don't stress if your friends make money on a company that you miss. Don't dwell on an idea that you didn't act on. In investing, there is always tomorrow, there is always the next opportunity. Keep reading, keep learning and keep your eye out for the next opportunity.

What to do when the market drops

At some point, it's going to happen. The market will drop and you'll see your investments lose value. Here's what to do in that situation.

Take a deep breath. Turn off the TV. Put your phone down. Do nothing.

It's an easy thing to say. It's a lot harder to do.

When markets fall, it is only natural to want to sell. You'll want to wait out the storm in a safe harbour but that is often the worst thing you can do.

Since 1990, there have been some famous market crashes. Less famous, but more important, are the market recoveries. In the past 30 years we've lived through the Asian financial crisis, the tech bubble bursting, the US housing market collapsing and Covid-19 shutting down the global economy.

Despite all of this turmoil, the value of the Australian stock market has more than tripled in that time.

Don't miss the recovery

The problem with selling after the market falls is that you miss out on the recovery. You sell at a low price and miss out as the market recovers.

As we've covered throughout *Get Started Investing*, the stock market is unbelievably resilient. No matter what the world has thrown at it—financial crisis, war, terrorist attacks, pandemics—it has rebounded. The reason it bounces back is because humans find a way to navigate these crises. Companies find ways to continue producing goods and services that people want to buy. Or in many cases, that people *need* to buy (think: services like Zoom video conferencing during the Covid-19 pandemic).

The Covid-19 pandemic and the stock market in 2020 give a great illustration of the power of just waiting.

The stock market falls and recovers—Covid-19 pandemic

Between late February and March 2020, the Australian stock market collapsed as fears about Covid-19 spread around the world.

If you had invested at the start of 2020, by the 23 March you would have lost one-third of your money. If you'd invested $1,000, you would have had only $666 left.

The worst possible thing you could have done is sold in late March.

Instead, if you'd controlled your fear and waited, your investments would have rebounded. On 24 November, the Australian stock market broke back to even for 2020. You would have had your full $1,000 back.

There is a lot to be said for doing nothing. In investing, it is often the best financial decision.

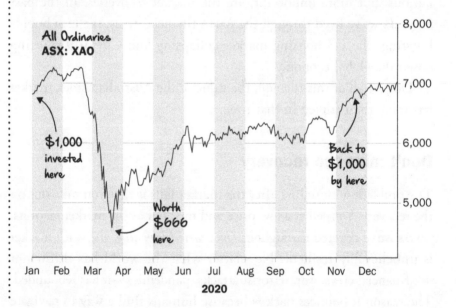

Don't sell; buy more

If 'don't sell' is the #1 rule, then a close second is 'buy more'. When markets fall, it creates a great buying opportunity for investors to buy at the bottom. That way, as the market recovers, you managed to buy at a great price.

If we build on the example of Covid-19 in 2020, you can see in the illustration how buying when the market falls can be a great investing strategy.

WARREN BUFFETT
fear, greed and bears

We keep returning to history's greatest investor, **Warren Buffett**, because he has a quote for every situation. Here's his philosophy when investors are fearful that markets are falling.

'Be fearful when others are greedy, and greedy when others are fearful.'

Benjamin Graham, the father of value investing and the author of some of the best investing books ever written, also had a great quote for when markets are falling (aka bear markets).

'Bear markets are when stocks return to their rightful owners.'

The stock market falls and recovers— Covid-19 pandemic continued

In our previous example, we explained how an investor who put $1,000 into the market at the start of 2020 would have lost one-third of their money by March and, if they waited, would have fully recovered their money by 24 November 2020.

Imagine our investor had another $1,000 to invest. If they had invested that money at the bottom of the market, on 23 March, that investment would have been up more than 50% by 24 November.

This means that the original $1,000 they invested would have broken even (i.e. back to $1,000) and the other $1,000 they invested would have turned into $1,500.

For an investor living through one of the toughest years for the economy in recent history, that would have been a great year.

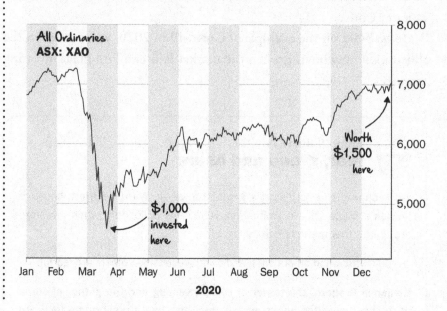

Section summary
YOUR PROGRESS

☑ BEYOND THE FIRST INVESTMENT

In this section we covered the art and science of portfolio construction. This is where the excitement of making your first investment turns into the long-term work of building a collection of investments that will build your wealth for decades to come.

You have:
- ✓ understood how to add money to your portfolio
- ✓ learnt about diversification
- ✓ prepared yourself for when the market drops and your portfolio is down
- ✓ understood why patience is a virtue when it comes to building long-term wealth.

PART 8

Lessons We Wish
We Had Known

We've learnt a lot of lessons the hard way over our journey of investing.
Take advantage of this and learn them the easy way in this section.

Be global

*It's a big world out there; technology has made it easy to
invest in it all.*

The past few years have seen an amazing improvement in access to stock markets around the world for Australian investors. Even as recently as 2015, when Alec started investing, it was difficult and expensive for everyday investors to access overseas markets. You were confined to investing in Australia. By 2018, Stake had launched in Australia, offering everyday investors free brokerage for US stocks.

Technology is breaking down the barriers to the world.

But too many Australians only invest in Australian stocks. This preference for investing in your home country is known as **home country bias.**

 PARDON THE JARGON
home country bias

Home country bias is the tendency for an investor to prefer companies from their own country or region. This leads to investors putting too much of their money in stocks from their home country.

Investing excessively in domestic stocks can create an unbalanced portfolio that has greater risk and can cause an investor to miss out on international investment opportunities.

There's nothing wrong with investing in Australian companies. We have some excellent companies and generations of investors have retired comfortably investing in only Australian companies.

We just think the world is a better pool to fish from.

Think about what you use

We're writing this book on an American computer, wearing clothes made in Asia, drinking coffee grown in Brazil, listening to music from a British band on a music app developed in Sweden.

We are all global consumers and we should be global investors as well.

Think about what you're buying, what you're watching and what you're reading. How much of it is made in Australia by Australian companies?

Chances are, not too much.

Then think about some of the most amazing technologies being developed. Or think about the companies you admire, or read about in the news. Think about where the most brilliant entrepreneurs are coming from. There's not one country that has a monopoly on brilliant ideas, brilliant people or brilliant companies.

So why would you only invest in Australian companies?

The problem is that too many people around the world have a home country bias in their investing portfolios.

- The average Australian investor has 67% of their money in Australian stocks, despite Australia being 2% of the global stock market.
- The average American investor has 80% of their money in American stocks, despite the USA being 40% of the global stock market.
- The average Canadian investor has 59% of their money in Canadian stocks, despite Canada being just 3% of the global stock market.
- The average Japanese investor has 55% of their money in Japanese stocks, despite Japan being 7% of the global stock market.

avoid home country bias

Many of the expert investors we speak to caution against investing too much of your money in your home country.

Pete Matthew is a chartered financial planner in the UK and managing director of Jacksons Wealth Management. He explained how being overly exposed to your home market means you could be missing out on opportunity.

> 'Way too many investors are over exposed to their home market. The UK market is something like 6% of global stock markets by value. So for UK investors to have 50, 60, 70, even 100% of their investments in the UK is missing out on a whole lot of value.'

Matt Leibowitz is the founder of Australian online broker Stake. He shared why he looks to the USA for investing opportunities.

> 'International investing is really important for Australians . . . I can see now we're using an Apple product, probably search on Google, going home to watch Netflix, probably going to buy something on Amazon in the next month or so, probably an NVIDIA chip somewhere in there . . . Buy something on your Visa and MasterCard, these companies are listed overseas. You know, we've had Spotify and Dropbox recently list. It actually makes a lot more sense for Australians to be looking at what they understand. If they're going to invest in something they know, they should actually be investing in the company, and therefore starting with companies they know. And those companies do not list in Australia.'

How Australia measures up

To give you an idea of how Australia measures up, consider this: there are approximately 630,000 stocks traded globally and 2,200 stocks in Australia—meaning that we are less than 1% of the total number of stocks traded around the world.

Or another way to think about it: the global stock market is worth $70.8 trillion US dollars, and Australia's stock market is worth

$1.3 trillion US dollars—meaning that Australia's stock market is about 2% of the global stock market.

Meaning that there are plenty of options out there.

YOUR SLICE OF THE PIE

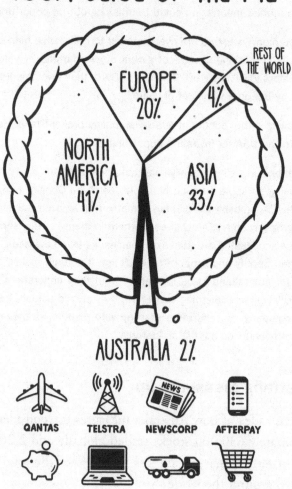

Those numbers are a little bit abstract. To give you an idea of the opportunity to invest overseas, the table shows how some of Australia's biggest companies measure up to their global competitors.

As investors, we have the opportunity to own some of the best companies in the world. We are not limited to our little corner of the world. We can invest globally.

Australia versus the world (all values in $AUD as of 31 March 2021)

Biggest supermarket	Woolworths • 1,024 stores • $64 billion revenue • Valued at $51 billion	Walmart • 11,510 stores • $720 billion revenue • Valued at $503 billion
Biggest tech companies	Afterpay • 7.3 million users • Valued at $29 billion	Apple • 1.4 billion users • Valued at $2.64 trillion
Biggest bank	Commonwealth Bank • 15.9 million customers • Valued at $152 billion	Industrial and Commercial Bank of China • 650 million customers • Valued at $400 billion
Biggest hospital operator	Ramsay Health Care • 72 hospitals and sites of care • Valued at $15 billion	HCA Healthcare • 2,184 hospitals and sites of care • Valued at $84 billion

Why the world is less risky

Being global isn't just important because of the opportunities we have overseas. It can also help us reduce the risk.

We've covered diversification in Part 5, but it's important enough to remind ourselves again. If all of your investments are in Australian companies and something goes wrong in the Australian economy, that means all of your investments will suffer. But if only a quarter of your investments are in Australia, then something going wrong in Australia will only affect a quarter of your portfolio.

If you think more broadly than just your stock portfolio, your job and your home are based in Australia. There's no way to diversify those two things away (unless you move). If something goes wrong in the Australian economy, your job may be at risk and the value of your home may fall. Owning overseas stocks means not everything is exposed to the performance of the Australian economy.

What are the best ways to access global markets?

There are plenty of ways to access global stocks:

- **Individual stocks:** Australians can sign up to online brokers that offer international stocks. You can buy shares in companies around the world from the comfort of your living room.
- **Index funds:** there are Australian funds that track foreign stock market indexes. For example, you can buy an Australian ETF that tracks America's S&P 500 index or the UK's FTSE 100 index.
- **Managed funds:** there are Australian-based professional investors who invest around the world or in specific foreign countries. You can put your money in their funds and have them invest around the world on your behalf.

No points for originality

This isn't school. In investing, copying the smart kids is encouraged!

We invest to make money. You don't make any additional money if you come up with an original idea, and you don't get any less money if you follow someone else.

In investing, there are no points for originality, so try to steal as many good ideas as you can.

The key caveat: if someone is wrong and you lose money, that's your loss. They are not responsible for your money. You need to do your own research and at the end of the day, make your own decisions.

There are no points for originality, but it's also no excuse if you're copying.

The best investors are always on the lookout for the best ideas out there, constantly reading, listening, observing and making lists of other people's best stock ideas to research themselves.

When we started investing, we had this idea that we had to come up with 'new' ideas. Find companies that no one had heard of before. We had this idea that the best investors were finding 'no name' companies. Over the years, we've learnt that isn't the case. Many of the best investors are investing in companies you've heard of and probably use.

Two of the best investors in the world are Bill Ackman, founder and CEO of Pershing Square Capital Management, an American fund manager, and Hamish Douglass, co-founder and chief investment officer of Magellan Financial Group, an Australian fund manager.

These are some of the companies Bill Ackman owns:

- Chipotle
- Hilton Worldwide
- Lowes
- Restaurant Brands International (owner of Tim Hortons, Burger King, Popeyes)
- Starbucks.

And these are some of the companies Hamish Douglass owns:

- Alphabet (Google)
- Facebook
- Microsoft
- Starbucks
- Tencent.

As you can see, these two multi-billion fund managers own companies that many people have used, and most people have heard of. Forget the idea that you need to find an unknown company, one that no one else has heard of.

Where do I find ideas?

The great news is there are plenty of resources online that can help you find stock ideas. Here are a few of our favourites.

- **Investor letters:** a large number of professional investors write quarterly or annual letters to their investors sharing their views on markets and any companies they've been researching. These letters are usually shared online for anyone to read. If you're looking for an investor to start with, search for Warren Buffett's investor letters. You really can't go past the greatest investor of all time.

- **Fund filings:** many professional investors are required by regulators to file monthly or quarterly updates that often include some of their biggest investments. In Australia, listed investment companies are required to release monthly fund updates to the public. In the USA, the largest investment funds are required to do something similar (in the USA, these forms are called 13Fs).
- **Online forums:** there are plenty of online forums where everyday investors are sharing ideas and analysis. You always need to be careful about these forums, and do your own research, but they can be a great source for ideas. Some of our favourites include Strawman, Twitter, Reddit and Facebook groups.

What to do once you have a list of ideas

Always do your own research. Never blindly follow someone else's idea.

You may be following a professional investor into an investment, but what if something changes and that investor sells the stock? They don't have to tell you. Or what if they're wrong and you notice something that they've overlooked?

Use other people's ideas to form a list of opportunities to research and look into yourself.

FROM THE EXPERTS
the best stock to buy

Andrew Page, the founder and managing director of Strawman.com, reminded us of the importance of investing in what you know and doubling down on your best ideas.

> 'There's no extra points for novelty in investing. And there's no extra points for degree of difficulty . . . When you study the great investors, most of their returns come from a small subset of their total selections and they just become super intimate with that stock in terms of understanding it, which gives them a real edge in investing. And that is a source of advantage that I think too many people ignore. So I know back in The Motley Fool days,

when we were running a newsletter, people just wanted something new all the time. Which always struck me as strange. I would imagine that what you want is the best idea. Even if it's the same idea and I forget who said it—might have [been] Peter Lynch who said that the best stock to buy is probably one that you already own.'

Be different

If you want to make money no one else is making, you've got to be
willing to do something no one else is doing.

This lesson isn't for everyone. As we explain throughout *Get Started Investing*, there is nothing wrong with getting market average returns. Since 1900, the Australian stock market has averaged returns of 13% a year. You can get rich and retire very comfortably averaging 13% a year.

For those who are looking to do better than average, you have to do something different from the average.

While market indexes have been a great innovation, they are by no means the best.

 FROM THE EXPERTS
the problem with indexes

In his book *Millennial Money*, **Patrick O'Shaughnessy**, the CEO of O'Shaughnessy Asset Management, wrote about the problems with standard market indexes.

> 'The primary weakness of market index products is that they have the investment strategy backward. Owning more of a company just because it is bigger than others is a bone-headed way to build a portfolio. Even stupid strategies can beat a market-capitalisation-weighted index. If you bought all large stocks in the United States that started with the letter C, you'd have outperformed the S&P 500 by 0.5% per year since 1962.'

The great thing for investors who want to be different and beat the market is that index investors have subbed out of the competition.

They aren't trying to beat the market average any more. Instead of trying to find the best companies, they've chosen to just own a bit of all of them. In theory, this should give more opportunity for those seeking to find those gems of companies and beat the market average. As Warren Buffett asked in his 1985 shareholder letter, 'What could be more advantageous in an intellectual contest—whether it be bridge, chess or stock selection—than to have opponents who have been taught that thinking is a waste of energy?'

If you're looking to be different, here are some steps you can take.

- Don't just invest in countries or companies that have done well in the past (as Warren Buffett said, 'if past history was all there was to the game, the richest people would be librarians').
- Think about industries that are being disrupted and the companies that are leading this disruption. The biggest and best companies of tomorrow won't be the biggest of today.
- Look for excellent entrepreneurs and company leaders. In many cases it is the people leading the businesses who make all the difference.
- Find companies that are investing in research and development and new business opportunities. Companies like CRISPR Therapeutics and Tesla are constantly looking at new ways to innovate and new opportunities for growth.

FROM THE EXPERTS
the importance of disruptive companies

Nick Griffin is the chief investment officer of Munro Partners. He spoke to us about the importance of finding those truly exceptional companies that are on the edge of an industry disruption.

'When you're investing in an equity, you're generally investing in someone's vision. Someone's idea. That could be truly great or it could fail spectacularly. And the key thing to remember is the vast majority fail spectacularly.

We could show you some analysis and it'd be the same in Australia or anywhere else in the world. But if you looked at the US market over the last 90 years, there's actually been 25,500 companies listed and more than 14,000 of them have gone to zero. So 60% of all companies go to zero. The next 8,000 only make enough to offset what the other 14,000 lose. And you end up with just 1,000 companies—so less than 4% of every company that list create the entire value of the US stock market.

And out of those 1,000 companies—if you take the top 50 of those 1,000 companies, they make up nearly 50% of that value. So 50 companies out of 25,000 when you started make up nearly 50% of the value. And so we know who those companies are now. We know who they are. They're Microsoft, they're Amazon, they're Google, they're Apple, you know, Home Depot, they're Walmart.

But what's interesting about them is there's usually a couple of strong individuals behind it and there's usually a structural disruption or a structural change that they're looking to exploit. And obviously, everyone's now focused on tech and I'm sure we'll end up talking about it. But if you go back over time, it was always something that was happening, whether it was big-box retailing creates Walmart and Home Depot, or quick service restaurants creates McDonald's, or entertainment creates Disney or air travel creates Boeing. But what's interesting about it is there are always only a few winners. Right. So, you know, thousands of companies tried to build a plane, but there's only two companies that can build a plane that you and I will knowingly get on: Airbus and Boeing.

Once you understand that is your philosophy, you realise that equity investing is actually about just going out and trying to find these exceptional companies.'

Just as important as what to do is what not to do. You won't find different companies in the news or financial media. Thousands, if not millions, of people will be reading the same news reports and watching the same financial news.

To find truly different companies you need to do your own research. One excellent tool that we've already touched on—but is valuable enough that we're going to double down—is a 'stock screener'. A stock screener starts with all companies available to invest in, and then lets you filter on your chosen metrics. You can filter by country, by industry or by different metrics. Want to only find companies that have grown their profit for the past five years? You can filter for that. Or if you want to only find companies that have zero debt, you can filter for that.

If you want to find stocks no one has heard of before, forget reading the news and find a stock screener instead.

Get out of your own way

People have a habit of making the right decision, overthinking it and then changing their mind. For investors, one of the most important things we can do is control our emotions and just get out of our own way.

The human brain is a fickle thing. Despite being so powerful, it can often lead us into mental mistakes.

One of the biggest lessons we've learnt is the importance of controlling your emotions. Making fast, rash decisions, changing your mind at the last minute or not acting because you're scared of losing money can lead to some devastating losses.

Understanding who you are as an investor is key. Understanding how your brain subconsciously works is also important. We all have some **cognitive biases** that we need to be aware of, so we can avoid their traps.

 PARDON THE JARGON
cognitive bias

A **cognitive bias** is a systematic error in thinking that occurs when people are processing and interpreting information in the world around them.

Unsure about that definition? Basically—our brains aren't perfect. They often make mistakes when taking in information from the world and trying to make sense of it. A cognitive bias is a term for these mistakes our brains often make.

The best example of a cognitive bias is investing based on FOMO (fear of missing out). If everyone else is making money on a stock and you're not, you'll very quickly feel left out. You'll often feel compelled to buy. Not because it's a good investment, but because everyone else is making money.

Beware FOMO investing—a cryptocurrency investment

 ALEC

In 2017, the investing world went cryptocurrency mad. Everyone was talking about, and investing in, Bitcoin and other cryptocurrencies. There were new cryptocurrencies being released every week and investors were making a lot of money in a very short period of time on these coins.

I resisted the crypto trend for most of 2017. I didn't understand cryptocurrency and where the value was, so I chose to keep my money in stocks.

But a lot of my friends were making money in crypto. Our group chat was filled with talk of crypto and the different coins my friends were investing in.

Eventually, FOMO got the better of me. Right at the end of 2017, I put some money into Bitcoin. That was the top of the market and over the next year, Bitcoin lost three-quarters of its value.

This was a reminder of the perils of FOMO investing. I got caught up in how everyone else was making money and didn't stick to my convictions.

I hope other investors can learn from my mistake here, and avoid investing because other people are making money.

Traditional economics and finance research assume that all humans are rational consumers. That we are good judges of value and our ability to be rational makes the markets efficient. Two psychologists, Daniel Kahneman and Amos Tversky, challenged this and introduced the concept of behavioural economics. Their basic premise was that our cognitive biases often led us to make economically irrational decisions.

This work has sparked a number of incredibly simple experiments that demonstrate our cognitive biases. We love some of these examples, so we're including some of them here.

- Experienced radiologists were asked to evaluate an X-ray as normal or abnormal, and then were asked to re-evaluate it. They contradicted their previous answer 20% of the time. Showing how we can inconsistently evaluate the same set of facts.
- When asked, most participants would prefer to receive a sure $46 than have a 50% chance of making $100. This, according to traditional economic theory, is irrational. The risk-weighted return (i.e. is it worth taking the risk based on the possible reward?) on the $100 is the rational choice. Showing how most people don't properly assess risk and reward when it comes to their finances.
- In a study, half of the participants were told the survival rate for surgery was 90%; the other half were told that the mortality rate was 10%. When asked if they would be willing to have the surgery, more of the 90% group said 'yes'. Showing how the same information presented in a different way can affect how we think about something.
- Participants observed a roulette wheel, half seeing it stop on the number 10, the other half seeing it stop on the number 65. They were then asked what percentage of United Nation countries are African. Those who saw the number 10 guessed 25% on average, whereas those who saw 65 guessed 45% on average. The results here show how our brains anchor to numbers we've recently seen, even if completely unrelated to the task or question at hand.
- In a study, half of the participants were given a mug and asked how much they'd sell it for; the other half were asked how much they'd buy it for. Those with a mug overestimated its value—the average answer being $5.78—whereas the average buyer would only pay $2.21. Showing we overestimate the value of things we already own.

- If a coin is flipped five times and lands heads all five times, most people believe it will land on tails on the next flip. But it is still a 50–50 chance. Showing how history can affect our ability to forecast future outcomes.

- When asked if people would prefer to have $150 today or $180 in one month, people tend to choose the $150 today. Giving up a 20% return in one month is an economically irrational choice. Showing that humans don't assess the time value of money like the economics textbooks say we do.

All of these studies demonstrated that humans are not perfectly rational. That, for a variety of reasons, our brains can make mistakes when processing information. The fact that humans are not perfectly rational means as investors we need to try to control our irrationality. We need to get out of our own way.

What are some of the key cognitive biases?

While there are many that we could discuss, we've pulled out a few that are related to investing. Every human is susceptible to them, so don't be alarmed if you think of instances where you've shown them. We definitely have. The key isn't to not have these biases; the important thing is to be aware of them and control them.

Confirmation bias

Where you put the conclusion first, and then seek out information to support and confirm your view. You pay attention to information that supports beliefs that are pre-existing, and don't consider information that challenges your thesis. How can you make proper decisions if you are not considering all available information?

Loss aversion

Do you find that losing money often evokes a stronger emotional response than making money? This is loss aversion. It's where you will feel more strongly about a loss than you do any gain of the same amount. In other words, you hate losing $100 more than you do gaining $100. This can lead to you selling winners (to lock in that profit) and holding losers (to avoid that feeling of loss).

Dunning–Kruger effect

Put simply, it's where you think you are better than you are! It's a bias in which people overestimate their ability at a particular task. In this case, it's where you feel like you're better at investing than you actually are. As a result, you might take on more risk or make decisions beyond what you truly understand.

Choice overload

Ever sit down at a restaurant that has 55 things on the menu and you struggle to decide what to get? This is choice overload. Making decisions is difficult when you are faced with many choices, and this is certainly relevant to investors. With thousands of stocks to choose from around the globe there is a tendency to either:

- buy everything, through an index
- buy nothing at all
- buy what is popular.

Availability heuristic

Has anyone ever asked you what your favourite movie is and you've answered with one that you most recently watched, even though it's not *really* your favourite? This is 'availability bias'. It's where your brain takes a shortcut ('heuristic' is a fancy word for a mental shortcut) and relies on the most recent of examples when evaluating decisions, or topics. You might make an investing decision based on recollections of recent news headlines or conversations with mates, rather than digging deeper to understand more.

Herding

Perhaps one of the most common cognitive biases you might experience. Herding is following the group, and basing your investing decisions on what everyone else is doing. If everyone is buying Bitcoin, and it's all over the news, you might feel like you're missing out, and jump on board. Herding can lead to the formation of asset bubbles (where prices go way beyond what an asset is worth)—and a lot of pain when they burst.

FROM THE EXPERTS
work hard to counteract cognitive bias

Ted Richards is a former AFL footballer and now director of business development at Six Park. Ted has spent time at Harvard University studying behavioural finance. We asked him about some of the common cognitive biases we need to be wary of as investors.

'These biases affect us all. It's who we are and how we think. These biases and heuristics have been important to ensure that we evolved over thousands of years but they weren't designed for modern investing. So things like loss aversion, where the power of losses are twice as powerful as the feeling you get when you gain something—are so important to be aware of with investing, because the reality is the market pretty much goes up half the time. And every other day the market's down.

So if you're checking your portfolio every day, you'll feel those losses far more than the ups, which could make you nervous and pessimistic, and that could influence your decision making.

The Dunning–Kruger effect. I feel like it's so important for investors because people can assess their ability to be greater at something than they actually are. When it comes to investing, especially males, often confidence can actually peak in our mid-twenties. If you listen to Charlie Munger and Warren Buffett speak in their updates over at Omaha—Charlie Munger, who's one of the best investors of all time, and what is he, 95 years old?—there were so many questions that came through [from the annual Berkshire Hathaway Annual General Meeting] in those seven or eight hours where he answered "I don't know." I think that honesty is so refreshing to see, as many investors talk like they have a crystal ball.

But the main one that I'd like to touch on is confirmation bias, which is really hard to sidestep. It's where we put a conclusion first, and then we search for all the evidence to support that conclusion, and then we discount anything that disagrees with that. And that's not just relevant to investing, that's relevant to all sorts of things, including politics.

Confirmation bias affects fund managers, and they know this, so what they often do is seek out the information that disagrees with them just to ensure that they're not being affected by confirmation bias.'

How can we get out of our own way?

There are a few things we've learnt over our journey that help us stay out of our own way:

- Have a rules-based approach: setting some rules (how often you'll invest, how much you'll invest, what you'll invest in) ahead of time will stop you making rash decisions in the moment. It'll stop you responding to the news of the day, or whatever hot stock is being discussed in the news or in your group chat.

- Keep an investing journal: every time you invest, taking the time to write down why you invested is a great habit to get into. It doesn't need to be an essay—it could be five, fifty, five hundred words. Just putting pen to paper (or fingers to keyboard these days) will mean you have a record of it. If you make money or lose money, you can look back and see why you invested in the first place and learn from that investment.

- Don't overtrade: there are a lot of factors that are encouraging our brains to constantly trade. The firehose of information, the daily news, the constantly moving stock prices—all encourage activity. As a thought experiment, imagine if every homeowner received a text every hour with the price they could sell their house for. There would be a lot more buying and selling of houses. Resisting these urges to constantly buy and sell is an important skill to learn.

- Continue to adopt a mindset of long-term investing.
- Forget the idea of getting rich quick.
- Wait to take action if you're feeling emotional: give it two days, seven days, ten days, then review.
- Look for others opinions and ideas that might contradict yours.
- Be in control of the noise: what information is worth listening to? What is just fuelling your emotion?
- If the stock is just not performing, then take the loss. 'I'll just wait until it gets back to the price it was when I bought it' is a common phrase we always hear. There are no guarantees. Let your winners run, and don't be scared of accepting a loss and moving on.
- Be patient: wait, just wait. Take your time to do your research. Consider your buy and sell decisions. Weigh up your options. It's a simple piece of advice but one that is often hard to practise. Try to get past that initial impulse to act and consider your decisions. Kahneman, the psychologist, discussed this initial impulse and then the more considered thought that follows as 'System 1 versus System 2 thinking'.

Explaining System 1 versus System 2

Daniel Kahneman introduced the idea that the brain can be divided into two separate systems:

- System 1 is the brain's fast, automatic, intuitive approach. System 1 involves the innate, subconscious mental activities that we're born with or that we develop as we grow.
- System 2 is the brain's slower, analytical approach where reason dominates. Usually, System 2 is activated when we are doing something that does not come naturally, meaning some sort of conscious mental activity is required.

ILLUSTRATING SYSTEM 1 VERSUS SYSTEM 2

A commonly used example to demonstrate the difference between System 1 and System 2 thinking is the following thought experiment:

A bat and a ball together cost $1.10. The bat costs $1 more than the ball.
How much does the ball cost?

The majority of people instantly guess the ball costs 10 cents. But the correct answer is 5 cents (and the bat cost $1.05). Most people work this out after thinking for a second, but their instant thought is 10 cents.

The fast, intuitive reaction of 10 cents is our System 1 brain reacting instantly. The slower, more considered and ultimately correct answer of 5 cents is a product of our System 2 brain taking over and considering it.

As investors, we want to ensure we're being led by our System 2 brain rather than our System 1.

FROM THE EXPERTS
understand temptations in order to avoid them

Meir Statman is the Glenn Klimek Professor of Finance at Santa Clara University. His research focuses on behavioural finance.

We asked Meir what was the one thing that he thought more investors should understand or a common thing that a lot of investors are currently getting wrong.

'People know that they have to save money. People know that they have to calibrate their spending. It is really on the investment side that people tend to make mistakes . . . The first thing is to recognise the kinds of cognitive errors that you are likely to encounter.'

We then asked Meir to give us an example of a cognitive error that we may come across.

'One is hindsight. That is, people look back, for example, at a stock that has done really well or a mutual fund, the money manager has done very well. And they say, "I just knew it, I just knew it." And people look back at 2007 and they say, "I just had a hunch in 2007, it is time to get out of the market."

But if you ask them to write in permanent ink their hunches about the future, you will find that their knowledge is zero. Not only do individual investors have zero foresight, professionals have zero foresight. It's embarrassing to see what Wall Street strategists forecasted in 2007 about what would happen in 2008. They had no clue.

And so don't try to time the market. Not only don't have hunches, but also stay away from this notion that they are going to be a contrarian because in every market, half the people think it is going to go up and half the people think it's going to go down. You'll never have a situation where everybody is exuberant or everybody is fearful.

So the thing really is to control your own exuberance and your own fear that is going to drive you out of the market or into the market, injuring yourself. Just be steady.'

 FROM THE EQUITY MATES
community

We asked members of the Equity Mates community what the hardest part about starting to invest was.

'You don't know what you don't know. I had a lot of peasant and working-class beliefs around money. I didn't have the psychology of a wealthy person and most of my friends were "working rich", buying holidays and brand-name clothing instead of investing. The first step for me was doing inner emotional work to change my mentality. I did that by becoming aware of my assumptions and deliberately challenging them. Emotions are a good indication that you need to pay attention to something. If I got upset when my husband challenged an assumption, instead of letting my emotion control me, I became curious and started asking myself questions to better understand my thoughts, emotions and behaviours. I would then do research, learning from people smarter and more experienced than myself to explore multiple perspectives. After that, my partner and I would discuss it. Together, we chose which beliefs served us and which we needed to change. There is a great saying, "You are not entitled to your opinion. You are entitled to your informed opinion. No one is entitled to be ignorant."—Harlan Ellison. When it came to money, I was often choosing ignorance. Developing informed opinions was hard work!'
AMANDA

'Recognising to take your emotions out of investing, particularly when the market has a bad day.'
MARK

'Emotional investing. Trial and error helped me to understand sometimes patience is key and for long-term investing, it can be counterproductive to watch the market daily unless led to believe there is reason to.'
NAOMI

Keep it simple

Too much sleep has been lost over analysing investment options.
Keep it simple and focus on the bigger picture.

Patrick O'Shaughnessy wrote in his book *Millennial Money,* 'As the saying goes, if you torture data long enough, it will tell you whatever you want to hear.'

This was a big learning for us in our investing journeys. It's easy to fall into the trap of thinking you need to analyse every data point. After all, it is your hard-earned money on the line.

The reason this is a trap is that you lose sight of the bigger picture. At the end of the day, remember what investing is all about—becoming a part-owner in a business and owning the business as it works to sell more products or services, generate more profit and reinvest that profit into growing further. If you focus on finding excellent businesses, then a lot of these other concerns become secondary.

As O'Shaughnessy continued in his book, the more you torture data the more you can find some strange correlations.

> This is crucial, because plenty of things predict market returns but make zero sense. For example, if you consider butter production in Bangladesh alongside sheep population in New Zealand, you can 'predict' 99% of the S&P 500's return between 1981 and 1993. This is a remarkably high correlation, but it doesn't mean we should buy the S&P 500 when butter production spikes.

As investors, it's important to focus on the big picture and keep it simple.

Keep it simple checklist: a few key things we focus on

- Do you understand what the company does and how it makes money?
- Is the company better than its competitors?
- Is the industry the company in growing or is there opportunity for it to grow in the future?
- Has the company been growing its customer or user numbers?
- Has the company been growing its revenue and profit?
- Is the company reinvesting this profit into growing its business and getting better at what it does?

Look for good management

Too often, investors look at companies as nameless, faceless brands. Always keep in mind that companies are collections of people and that the quality of the people and the culture of the company is one of the most important factors in finding good investments.

There have been a lot of lessons we've picked up from the expert investors we've spoken to over our journey. One of the most important ones is to look at the quality of company management and the culture of the company.

It's understandable why we forget to think about people and culture. We often think about these companies as the stock tickers they trade under. Woolworths is WOW, Telstra is TLS and ZipPay is Z1P. At the same time, financial media report on companies as though they are their own thinking, acting organisms. 'Afterpay expands services to America', 'Blue Sky has misstated its financial position', 'Wesfarmers buys Coles Supermarkets'.

We cannot forget what sits behind these company decisions. People. Every day the people who work at these companies are making decisions. They are weighing up the pros and cons of different options, trying to understand what their customers want and reacting to what their competitors are doing.

When we say 'Afterpay expands services to America' we're actually saying that the leadership team at Afterpay has made a decision to invest money in expanding to the USA. That the managers are going to send people over to set up an office, hire new employees in the USA and work hard to acquire customers and grow its business over there. The success of that decision is not preordained. It cannot be said to be a 'good' or 'bad' decision at the time. The success will be determined by the employees the company tasks with making this American expansion happen. Their effort, their ingenuity and their results are what will determine success.

The difference between a really successful company and a so-so company is often the quality of their people. Those managers who can solve big problems and have a vision for the future are often able to bring their companies through difficult situations that would crush other businesses.

As investors, understanding a company's people and culture is a really useful piece of information.

FROM THE EXPERTS
you are really investing in people

Ed Cowan is a former Australian Test cricketer and a member of the Investment Team at TDM Growth Partners. He shared with us why people are so important when making investing decisions.

'The investment philosophy that comes out more than anything is we are investing in people to allocate capital on our behalf. When you own the business, you are backing the CEO, you're backing the board and you're backing the senior executives to grow these businesses over long periods of time. And getting the people right is just such a key tenet of what we believe.'

Leadership starts at the top, thinking about the CEO

CEO stands for chief executive officer. They are the leader of the business. Ultimately responsible for the day-to-day operations of the company, they have more to do with the success or failure of your investment than almost anyone else.

The best investors, and the best analysis, can all come undone if the CEO isn't able to execute their business plans.

The difference a CEO can make

STEVE JOBS AND APPLE

There is no better example of the importance of a visionary CEO than the world's biggest public company, Apple. Today Apple is worth over $2 trillion, but this success was not always guaranteed.

Steve Jobs and Steve Wozniak founded Apple in 1976, originally working out of Jobs' parents' garage. Despite some early success, and publicly listing in 1980, by 1985 Jobs was on the outer and resigned from Apple.

In his time away from Apple, Jobs founded NeXT Computers (a commercial failure, but the computer upon which the World Wide Web was invented) and co-founded Pixar (the animation studio responsible for films such as *Toy Story*, *Monsters Inc.* and *Finding Nemo*).

While Jobs was away from Apple the company was suffering. Bill Gates' Microsoft was taking its market share and Apple was undergoing extensive layoffs and cost cutting. When Jobs was brought back to the company in 1997, Apple was only weeks away from bankruptcy.

After Jobs returned to Apple, it developed a string of successful products—the iMac, the iPod and then the iPhone.

Between the start of 1985 and when Jobs returned in February 1997, Apple's share price was only up 15%—a long twelve years for Apple shareholders. In the twelve years after Jobs returned to Apple, the share price was up 4800%. Such a remarkable turnaround for a company that was on the edge of bankruptcy is a classic example of how instrumental a CEO can be to the fortunes of a company.

ROBERT IGER AND DISNEY

Disney is a cultural phenomenon, a company that is well known throughout the world. With a stable of incredibly powerful intellectual property—Mickey Mouse, Simba, Buzz Lightyear—it is one of those companies that you would expect to succeed whoever is at the helm.

But in the early 2000s Disney was struggling. It suffered through a string of poorly performing movies (anyone remember *Meet the Robinsons*?) and saw its competitors successfully move into computer animation—Dreamworks with *Shrek* and Pixar with *Monsters Inc.* and *Finding Nemo*.

At one stage, Disney had been working with Pixar on movies, including *Toy Story* and *A Bug's Life*, but relationships between Disney's CEO Michael Eisner and Pixar's co-founder Steve Jobs lead to a split between the two companies in 2004.

At the same time, Disney failed in its attempt to take over Universal Studios and Walt Disney's nephew Roy E. Disney and CEO Michael Eisner had a very public falling out. All was not well at Disney.

In 2005, Michael Eisner resigned and Bob Iger became CEO of the entertainment giant. Iger managed to turn Disney around and make it into an even bigger giant. He mended the relationship with Pixar before acquiring the company in 2006. He also acquired Marvel, LucasFilms (think: *Star Wars*) and 20th Century Fox. He expanded the company's footprint in China, opening Shanghai Disneyland, and entered the streaming business with Disney+.

In the fifteen years before Iger took over (1990–2005), Disney's share price was up 200%. In the fifteen years under Iger's leadership (2005–2020) Disney's share price was up almost 500%. That's the difference a great CEO can make.

The importance of a great CEO cannot be understated. Here are a few tips and tricks we've picked up along our journey to help you think about a company's CEO.

- **Look at their track record**: many CEOs have led other companies before their current job. How did they perform? Did they successfully grow the company? Or if they have been in their current job for a while, how has the company performed under their leadership? Have they outperformed expectations?
- **Long-term thinker**: the best CEOs are long-term thinkers. They don't care what the share price will do today or tomorrow, they care about how their business will be positioned five, ten, twenty years from now. Read their public statements and see how they're talking and what they're focused on.

- **What are the CEO's values**: does the CEO have a set of values that are motivating them? The CEO's values will often become the company's values and will form the basis of their vision for the company's future. Visionary CEOs are often able to articulate a clear vision that drives the company forward, such as Amazon's Jeff Bezos wanting to be the world's most customer-centric company or Tesla's Elon Musk wanting to accelerate the advent of sustainable transport by bringing compelling mass-market electric cars to market as soon as possible.
- **How is the CEO compensated**: the amount CEOs get paid often makes headlines. As an investor, worry less about what they get paid and focus more on why they get paid. Every CEO will have performance targets set by the company's board. These performance targets dictate how much a CEO will get paid, so they have significant personal incentive to meet or exceed the targets set.
- **Do they have skin in the game**: CEOs who own shares in the companies they run have their personal fortunes tied to the performance of the company. It ensures they are aligned with you as a shareholder, and will make decisions in the best interest of shareholders. Just be mindful that some CEOs will try and get a short-term 'sugar hit' for their share price and then sell their stock. Always watch out for that.

Over our journey, we've come across some good advice on how to spot a great CEO. These three books are our top picks for advice on identifying the best leaders:

- *The Outsiders: Eight Unconventional CEOs and Their Radically Rational Blueprint for Success* by William Thorndike
- *The Hard Thing About Hard Things: Building a Business When There Are No Easy Answers* by Ben Horowitz
- *Sam Walton: Made in America* by Sam Walton.

One final note: there is a trend emerging around the length of time CEOs are staying at one company. During the second half of the 20th century, CEOs often held their posts for ten to fifteen years. But in the first decade of the 21st century, the average tenure for CEOs at the world's 2500 largest public companies fell from 8.1 years to 6.3 years.

There's nothing that can be done about this. This is the nature of the short-term focus of markets (and we guess the world . . .). It is just something to keep in mind when looking at the CEOs of the companies you invest in.

The real work is done by the workers—understanding the corporate culture

Perhaps even more important that the CEO who is leading a company is the culture at a company. When we talk about company culture, we're talking about the values, goals, attitudes and practices that characterise an organisation. It captures the way people feel about the work they do, the values they share, where they see the company going and what they're doing to get there.

Culture is important for a number of reasons. Chief among them, it can often determine the quality of talent it can attract. The best workers in the world have options when it comes to where to work, and the companies with the best teams are often able to succeed where others wouldn't. Ensuring that your company has the right culture to attract the best talent should be priority #1 for any business leader.

Famous examples of company culture

ZAPPOS

The online shoe retailer has become almost as famous for its company culture as for the shoes it sells. When hiring new candidates, the company does a specific 'cultural fit' interview, which carries half the weight of whether a candidate is hired.

Once hired, new employees are offered $2,000 to quit after the first week of training if they decide that the job isn't right for them.

SOUTHWEST AIRLINES

In an industry known for overworked, tired team members, Southwest Airlines is known for its happy and friendly employees who try hard to help. This starts at the top, as management works hard to communicate its goals and vision to make all employees feel part of a unified team. Managers also empower employees, giving them permission to go the extra mile to make customers happy and do what they need to do to meet their vision of the 'most loved' airline.

ADOBE

The US software giant is focused on building a culture that trusts and empowers employees. It avoids micromanaging, and gives employees challenging projects and trusts them to meet those challenges.

The company works to foster creativity throughout its teams and ensures managers are giving teams the space to feel truly free to create. One example of this: Adobe does not use ratings to establish employee capabilities or in performance reviews, feeling that it inhibits creativity and how teams work. Instead, Adobe managers are expected to take on the role of a coach, and help employees set goals and determine how they should be assessed.

Not all companies seek to foster a 'warm and welcoming' company culture. Netflix is famous for its different take on what makes a 'good culture'.

NETFLIX

The online streaming giant may be the best-known example of company culture around the world. The company's original 'culture deck' slideshow was published online and Facebook COO Sheryl Sandberg praised it as 'the most important document ever to come out of the Valley'.

Netflix's culture prioritises 'people over process'. The company wants to develop a 'dream team' of only the best of the best people. Unusually, it gives 'okay performers' generous severance packages so that it can replace them with a superstar. It describes itself as a 'team' rather than a 'family' and explain it as such:

> We model ourselves on being a team, not a family. A family is about unconditional love, despite, say, your siblings' bad behavior. A dream team

is about pushing yourself to be the best teammate you can be, caring intensely about your teammates, and knowing that you may not be on the team forever.

To put this philosophy into practice, Netflix requires all managers to perform a 'keeper test'. Basically, if one of their team members was thinking of leaving for another firm, would the manager try hard to keep them from leaving? If the answer is no, then that employee isn't up to the standard they want.

Netflix also explicitly says, 'In the tension between honesty and kindness, we lean into honesty'. It takes this open and honest culture to an extreme by making almost every document, including performance reviews, open for any employee to read.

As an investor, it can often be hard to gauge the culture of a company. A 'good culture' is a broad term that can mean different things to different people. Even if there was a universal standard for 'good culture', there aren't any easy data points to understand which companies are good and which ones are not. But here are a few tips and tricks we've learnt along the way:

- **Employee review sites**: websites like Glassdoor offer employees the opportunity to share feedback on the companies they work for and give the best insight into the culture of particular companies. For example, at the time of writing, Google enjoyed a 4.5 star rating on Glassdoor whereas News Corp sat at 3.2 and Kraft Heinz sat at 2.7.
- **Company leadership**: review the public statements of company leaders and the social media pages and websites of companies themselves. They will often give an insight into the culture the company is seeking to build. For example, Netflix has a page on its website dedicated to explaining in detail its corporate culture and the reasons the company are trying to build it in that way.
- **Customer reviews**: reading reviews on sites like Yelp or Google gives some insight into how the company deals with the public. These always need to be taken with a grain of salt, as people who

have bad experiences are far more likely to take the time to write a review than those who have good experiences. But they can give some insight into the company's culture (e.g. Southwest Airlines, a company that wants to be the 'most loved' airline enjoys a 4.5 out of 5 rating on TripAdvisor, compared to 3 for United, 3 for America and 4 for Delta—its three major competitors).

People change, should my investments?

The challenge with looking at the people and culture of a business is that they change. As we noted above, CEOs are sticking around for shorter and shorter periods of time and as they change, the cultures of organisations change as well.

It's not just CEOs who are changing more frequently. The average Australian employee stays in one job for three years and four months and will change jobs twelve times throughout their life.

How should we think about long-term investing when people and culture aren't long term?

There are a few key things to keep in mind here.

- The first is that the best organisations will have the right processes in place to ensure effective succession planning and that good cultures endure.

- The second is that people and culture shouldn't be the be-all and end-all. The very best companies are those that are run by great people but could be run by terrible people; that have sustainable competitive advantages and are growing, but also happen to be run by excellent managers. As the famous investor Warren Buffett has said, 'I try to invest in businesses that are so wonderful that an idiot can run them. Because sooner or later, one will.'

- The final thing is just to pay attention as managers change. When a company announces a change of CEO, the market will often react to the news—either pushing the stock higher or lower depending on their thoughts on the new leader.

The ultimate popularity contest: Famous market reactions to new CEOs

Sometimes the market loves you:

- In 2019, Under Armour announced a new CEO, Patrik Frisk, and the share price rose 7%.
- In 2018, Chipotle announced it was replacing its founder with a new CEO, Brian Niccol, the former CEO of Taco Bell. The share price jumped 15%.

Sometimes the market doesn't:

- In 2005, AutoZone announced a new CEO, William C. Rhodes III, and the share price fell 13%.
- In 2014, Microsoft CEO Steve Ballmer announced his resignation and the share price rose 8%.

As companies change their leadership, make sure you're staying on top of the news and doing your research on the new team.

Get rich by reading

*There are plenty of ways to learn about finance and investing,
but none better than books. You've already read this far into one
investing book; in this section we're going to share a few more
suggested by the experts and the Equity Mates community.*

Notable Australian investor John Hempton was once asked about which
investing books he'd recommend. He responded, 'You do need to read
five [investing books]. It actually doesn't really matter which five' and
he followed it up with 'Pick five, any five'.

We love these quotes because it really sums up our view on reading
investing books. Among the vast number of books written on this
subject, you'll find a huge variety of views, perspectives and preferred
investing styles. There is no one book that is gospel. No one book has
all the answers. But there is a compounding power of knowledge.

Every investing book you read, you'll learn something new. As you
read more and more you'll synthesise ideas between different books and
build your own investing philosophy. It really is the best way to learn.

 FROM THE EQUITY MATES
community

What has been your biggest lesson since starting?

'Read/listen/gather as much information as I can in my free time.'
MICHAEL

There are two specific reasons we think books are the best way to learn about investing.

- **They are long term:** books by their nature are written to be timeless. They have been written to be relevant years from now, and this gives them a long-term focus. The lessons you pick up won't be about the 'hot stock of the day' or 'the next big industry'. They are centred on timeless investing principles and will help you build that all-important long-term focus.
- **They are written by the best:** some of history's greatest investors have shared the lessons they've learnt over a lifetime of investing in their books. It is the closest thing most of us will ever find to being mentored by the very best in the business. Books from some of the early 20th century's greatest investors, like Benjamin Graham and Jesse Livermore, are still recommended today. Reading books from some of these investors would be like getting a goal-kicking lesson from AFL legend Tony Lockett or a lesson in essay writing from Virginia Woolf. An opportunity not to be missed.

What books should you start with?

There are so many great investing books out there, this was a difficult section to write. We've included a few of our favourites and a few recommended by the experts in the Equity Mates community. If you're looking for more recommendations, we've got a page on the Equity Mates website (equitymates.com/recommended-books) with more. (Had to get a shameless plug in!)

We've broken these recommendations into three sections: books for the beginner investor; books for the more experienced investor; and books about business and entrepreneurship more generally. But there's no wrong way to read—pick titles that interest you or authors you admire. Just keep reading!

Books we recommend

Books to get you started

ALEC
Millennial Money by Patrick O'Shaughnessy
Warren Buffett's Ground Rules by Jeremy Miller
The Snowball by Alice Schroeder

BRYCE
Second vote for *Millennial Money* by Patrick O'Shaughnessy
Shareplicity by Danielle Ecuyer
One Up on Wall Street by Peter Lynch

Books for the more experienced investor

ALEC
Margin of Safety by Seth Klarman
The Intelligent Investor by Benjamin Graham
Market Wizards by Jack D. Schwager

BRYCE
The Most Important Thing by Howard Marks
Value.Able by Roger Montgomery
The Little Book That Still Beats the Market by Joel Greenblatt

Books about business and entrepreneurship

ALEC

Super Pumped by Mike Isaac

Sam Walton: Made in America by Sam Walton

Tools of Titans by Tim Ferriss

BRYCE

Shoe Dog by Phil Knight

The Ride of a Lifetime by Robert Iger

Factfulness by Hans Rosling

Are you investing or speculating?

This was a question that we first came across in Seth Klarman's book Margin of Safety *and it's stuck with us ever since.*

How do you expect to make money? That is the underlying question that Seth Klarman posed in the first chapter of his book *Margin of Safety*. Do you expect to make money because your investment generates cash or do you expect to make money because someone will pay more for it in the future?

Klarman wrote that there are two key categories of assets: investments and speculations.

- Investments generate cash flow for an investor. Examples include a machine that makes widgets that could be sold; a building occupied by tenants who pay rent; or a timber plantation that could one day be harvested.
- Speculations do not generate cash flow but move up and down in price. Examples include art; antiques; rare coins; gold and fine wine.

The difference between these two groups is not always clear. Both investments and speculations can be valuable, both can be bought and sold, both typically fluctuate in price. The key difference is that investments generate cash flow for their owners, speculations do not.

This distinction can be summed up as 'productive asset versus non-productive assets' or 'assets that create value versus assets that are valuable'. One group you can make money just by owning them (investments); the other group you can only make money when you sell them (speculations).

When you think of it like that, would you rather own property or a Picasso?

Applying this to the stock market

This distinction between investing and speculating can be applied to the stock market. There are investors who think of stocks like investments and those who think of stocks like speculations.

Investing

Investors focused on investing are focused on the fundamentals of a business. To them, stocks represent fractional ownership of the business and they buy when they think the business is poised for growth or is cheap. They expect to profit from the share price as the business grows, from dividends the business pays out or by the market realising the prospects for the company and narrowing the gap between share prices and underlying business value.

Speculating

Speculators, by contrast, are focused on the share price. They are less concerned with the fundamentals of the business and are instead focused on whether the stocks will move up or down in price. They are not predicting the future for a business but rather are trying to predict the behaviour of others, and what they'll pay for the share in the future.

In his book, Klarman tells a story about sardine traders that sums up that speculative mentality.

> There is the old story about the market craze in sardine trading when
> the sardines disappeared from their traditional waters in Monterey,
> California. The commodity traders bid them up and the price of

a can of sardines soared. One day a buyer decided to treat himself
to an expensive meal and actually opened a can and started eating.
He immediately became ill and told the seller the sardines were no
good. The seller said, 'You don't understand. These are not eating
sardines, they are trading sardines.'

Like sardine traders, many financial-market participants are
attracted to speculation, never bothering to taste the sardines they
are trading.

The issue with the speculator mentality is that you're playing a
psychological game. You're trying to predict how other people will
think about a stock in the future—how much people will be willing
to pay for something. That's a difficult game to play.

As Klarman neatly summed up:

Speculators are obsessed with predicting—guessing—the direction of
stock prices. Every morning on cable television, every afternoon on the
stock market report, every weekend in Barron's, every week in dozens
of market newsletters, and whenever business people get together,
there is rampant conjecture on where the market is heading. Many
speculators attempt to predict the market direction by using technical
analysis—past stock price fluctuations—as a guide. Technical analysis
is based on the presumption that past share price meanderings, rather
than underlying business value, hold the key to future stock prices.
In reality, no one knows what the market will do; trying to predict
it is a waste of time, and investing based upon that prediction is a
speculative undertaking.

Mark Twain once said, 'There are two times in a man's life when
he should not speculate: when he can't afford it, and when he can.'
We agree.

Your money can make a difference

Investing is often seen as a capitalist bloodsport, and companies are often seen as willing to do anything to increase their profit. What we've learnt is that there is a fast-growing 'ethical investing' movement that is trying to change all of that. There are oppor- tunities to use your money to make a difference while also making money. You can do good, while doing good.

As everyday people looking at the world, there's a lot we want to change and little ability to effect this change. Climate change is a particularly salient example. For years, decades even, we have looked at the Australian government's inability to form a consensus and tackle this problem head on, despite the overwhelming scientific consensus that something needs to be done.

Climate change may be the most salient example, but it is not the only one. Challenges around modern slavery, animal welfare and factory farming, environmental degradation, even gambling and poker machines are all issues that are front of mind for a lot of Australians, with little progress from governments and regulators.

Due to the political gridlock, many Australians have started looking to companies to take action on their own, not waiting for governments to change the law or regulators to change policies, but instead take a leadership position on a number of these issues. To invest in renewable energy and divest from fossil fuels. To better manage their supply chains and self-report on environmental, social and governance (ESG) issues.

For corporate leaders, this then creates a game theory problem. Many have been reluctant to take action if their competitors will not.

There is a growing movement hoping to break this gridlock and force companies to lead this change: the ethical investing movement.

Investors can make a difference

Companies rely on investors to help them raise money in the stock market. Company boards are elected by shareholders. When investors care about something, companies start caring about these things a lot more as well.

This has led to the rise of the **ethical investing** movement.

PARDON THE JARGON
ethical investing

Ethical investing is a movement of investors who only invest in companies that are 'ethical'. While ethics differ from person to person and country to country, key focuses of the ethical investing movement are action on climate change, ending modern slavery, and avoiding products and practices that harm human health, such as tobacco, alcohol and gambling.

Ethical investors also look at how companies treat their employees and look after their welfare. Basically, if a company is not acting responsibly and making ethical and sustainable decisions, then the company will not be getting their money.

There are some notable fund managers and super funds in Australia that are leading the ethical investment movement, including Australian Ethical Investments and Future Super. The Responsible Investment Association Australasia estimates that almost $1 trillion of Australian investor money is invested under some form of responsible or ethical framework. This is a massive step for a movement that was considered niche just five or ten years ago.

This movement is global and some of the biggest organisations in the world are joining the ethical investing movement.

Developments in the ethical investing sector

WORLD'S LARGEST FUND MANAGER JOINS

BlackRock is an American asset manager with more than $7 trillion dollars under management. In 2019 the CEO of BlackRock, Larry Fink, wrote a public letter announcing their commitment to invest ethically and sustainably. Here is an excerpt from that letter:

> 'Climate change has become a defining factor in companies' long-term prospects. Last September, when millions of people took to the streets to demand action on climate change, many of them emphasized the significant and lasting impact that it will have on economic growth and prosperity—a risk that markets to date have been slower to reflect. But awareness is rapidly changing, and I believe we are on the edge of a fundamental reshaping of finance . . .
>
> In a letter to our clients today, BlackRock announced a number of initiatives to place sustainability at the center of our investment approach, including: making sustainability integral to portfolio construction and risk management; exiting investments that present a high sustainability-related risk, such as thermal coal producers; launching new investment products that screen fossil fuels; and strengthening our commitment to sustainability and transparency in our investment stewardship activities.'

WORLD'S LARGEST SOVEREIGN WEALTH FUND JOINS

Sovereign wealth funds are funds set up by governments to manage wealth on behalf of a country. Australia has a sovereign wealth, the Future Fund, that manages almost $160 billion on behalf of the Australian Government.

The largest sovereign wealth fund in the world is Norway's; it manages more than $1 trillion. Despite much of this money being made from oil exports, the fund is committed to ethical investing. The fund will not invest in companies that do not meet their standards for children's rights, climate change, water management, weapons production and a number of other ethical areas.

This move towards ethical investing is driving some real change in how companies do business. We're seeing many companies now take the lead and take the action that many governments have been reluctant to take.

Successes of the ethical investing movement

It's all good and well to talk about the increase in ethical investing. However, the key question is, has it made a difference?

There are a few notable examples of companies turning their attention to the sustainability concerns of their shareholders, both in Australia and overseas.

Here are just a few examples of companies prioritising sustainability.

- RE100 is a global initiative working to get businesses to commit to 100% renewable electricity. For many companies, this is an expensive choice, but increased pressure from customers and shareholders has seen some of the biggest companies in Australia and around the world join the cause. Australian companies including Woolworths, Atlassian, Macquarie Group, Westpac, Suncorp, QBE, Mirvac, National Australia Bank and Dexus have joined a growing list of global companies involved, including Vodafone, Salesforce, 3M, Walmart, Tesco, Sony, Nestlé, Unilever, Visa, Starbucks, PepsiCo, Microsoft, Mars, Mastercard, LEGO Group, Lyft, Google, General Motors and Facebook.
- Project Gigaton, launched by Walmart in 2017, is an initiative to reduce greenhouse gas emissions by more than 1 billion tonnes by 2030. More than 200 of Walmart's suppliers have joined the effort and they have already reduced their greenhouse gas emissions by over 100 million tonnes.
- In 2017, Volvo was the first traditional car-marker to commit to electrifying its entire range. Every new Volvo is now released with at least one electric motor (e.g. either hybrid or electric) and is targeting 2025 for carbon-neutral manufacturing.

- Australian company Wesfarmers (owner of Bunnings, Kmart, Target, Officeworks among others) has been incorporating a 'shadow carbon price' into their investment decisions for years. This adds costs to business decisions that will create carbon emissions, making them less attractive financially. Globally, a 2017 *Harvard Business Review* study found that 1400 companies incorporate a carbon price into their investment decisions.

How can we as individuals participate in this movement?

The great news is you don't need to be a billion-dollar money manager to have your money contribute to the ethical investing movement. We, as everyday investors, can get involved in three main ways.

- **Individual stocks:** as an owner of an individual share in a company, you have the right to vote on a number of matters at an annual general meeting (AGM). Many people do not use these votes or attend these meetings. But we are able to allocate our votes to an ethical fund manager, who can then vote on our behalf.
- **ETFs and managed funds:** there are a number of ETFs and managed funds that only invest in ethical Australian and foreign companies that Australian investors can put their money with. The decisions these funds make about what companies are ethical and unethical can have an impact on company's share prices and create an incentive for companies to ensure they're staying on the ethical side of the ledger. By putting more of your money into these funds you increase this incentive for companies to stay on the right side of the ethical/ unethical divide.
- **Superannuation:** super is the biggest opportunity to support the ethical investing movement. The sheer size of super funds and the amount of money they have allow them to really drive the sustainability agenda forward. Similar to ETFs and managed funds, companies have an incentive to stay on the right side of the ethical/

unethical decisions of these super funds. Super funds can also invest in renewable energy projects and earn a return for investors while also transforming Australia's energy generation infrastructure. How do you actually use your super for good? Look up your super fund's website; it should have a sustainability policy. If it doesn't, or you don't like what you're reading, do your research and find a super fund that is investing in a way that is aligned with your values.

Look for a moat

Much like moats protected castles from invaders in the Middle Ages and moats protect celebrity homes from paparazzi in LA today, business moats are able to protect companies from their competitors.

A term you'll often hear in investing circles is 'look for businesses with **moats**'. For investors who want to invest in individual stocks, this is an incredibly important concept to understand.

 PARDON THE JARGON
moats

'**Moats**' is a shorthand term for long-term, sustainable competitive advantages. They are the reasons a business is protected from being disrupted by its competitors and able to hold on to or continue growing its market share.

The term was popularised by legendary investor Warren Buffett and he explained the term as follows:

> The key to investing is not assessing how much an industry is going to affect society, or how much it will grow, but rather determining the competitive advantage of any given company and, above all, the durability of that advantage. The products and services that have wide, sustainable moats around them are the ones that deliver rewards to investors.

Warren Buffett isn't the only investor to focus on the importance of moats. A number of other experts have said similar things.

FROM THE EXPERTS
the importance of moats

Phil Fisher was an American investor, active for more than 60 years, and author of *Common Stocks and Uncommon Profits*.

'A strong ability to defend established markets against new competitors is essential for a sound investment.'

Thomas Russo is a hedge fund manager and the managing member of Gardner Russo & Gardner.

'The best long-term margin of safety comes not from an investment's price but from the value of a company's competitive advantage.'

Charlie Munger is vice president of Berkshire Hathaway, the investment company of the legendary Warren Buffett.

'We buy barriers, we don't build them. Some industries simply don't have barriers to entry and never will so we avoid them.'

Brian Vollmer is a member of the senior investment team at Brown Brothers Harriman, one of the largest and oldest private banks in the USA.

'As research analysts, we spend most of our time understanding the competitive moat—we need confidence that those growing cash flows will not be competed away over time.'

Adam Smith was a Scottish economist and is known as the 'the Father of Economics'.

'Any company whose earnings are growing consistently or, more important, are likely to grow consistently has something unique about it. The competition can read these earnings records too, and fat earnings records are an invitation to come in and sample the cream. So a company that has something unique about it has something the competition cannot latch on to right away. Whatever it is that is unique is a glass wall around those profit margins.'

Chuck Akre is the founder, managing member, CEO and chief investment officer of Akre Capital Management, an asset management fund.

'Few businesses possess an "economic moat" formed by enduring competitive advantages. Our experience reinforces the fact that it is these moats which enable the businesses to earn higher returns on capital than average.'

Christopher Begg is the co-founder, CEO and chief investment officer of East Coast Asset Management, Inc.

'We devote probably 90% of our intellectual horsepower to understanding whether the competitive moat around the business is widening or narrowing.'

The different types of moats

There are a number of different types of moats out there. We've covered four of the most common to give you an idea of what a moat can look like.

1 Cost advantage

A cost advantage is when a company can produce a product significantly cheaper than its competitors. This might be because it has a new technology, a better manufacturing process or simply because it enjoys the benefits of scale (larger companies are able to buy in bulk and achieve lower prices as a result).

Examples of each are as follows:

- **New technology:** PepsiCo is using artificial intelligence and machine learning to improve its manufacturing process.
- **Process:** Toyota was able to take the global car market by storm in the 1970s with its new lean manufacturing process, which allowed it to offer a quality car at a lower cost than any of its rivals.
- **Scale:** Walmart is able to buy more than many of its competitors and gets a cheaper price as a result.

Companies with a cost advantage are able to price goods and services lower than their competitors or make more profit than their competitors and use that profit to reinvest in better products or services.

When thinking about cost advantage the most important question is: is it durable? The examples of Toyota and Walmart show that it is rarely the case. Walmart is now facing price challenges from Amazon and Costco, while Toyota's manufacturing methods have been studied and emulated across the world.

As an investor you have to look for companies that are using their cost advantage to its utmost potential while they still have it.

2 Network effect

A network effect occurs when all users of a good or service benefit from every additional user. Think about a company like Facebook, where its service becomes more valuable as more users sign up.

Companies that can build a network develop a moat, as their product already has the user base that makes it more valuable than the rival company. Take the Facebook example, and imagine trying to set up a competing social network site today. Facebook already has 2.5 billion monthly active users, but more importantly it has your family, your friends and your colleagues as members. For an individual to leave Facebook and go to a new social network, they'd lose the social aspect unless all their contacts came with them. This network effect makes companies that have it incredibly hard to disrupt.

Another company with an incredibly powerful network effect is Microsoft. Microsoft Office products (think: Microsoft Word, Excel and Powerpoint) are the standard for businesses and schools across the world. A rival software company may come out with a better word processor, but it's no good if no one can read the documents you send them because they don't have the software as well.

It's incredibly hard to break this network effect. Just imagine trying to convince the company you work for to stop using Microsoft Office.

3 Brand

A company's brand can convey trust or status or meaning. If customers like a company's brand, they'll stick with them regardless of how many competitors enter the market. Think about a company like Nike. Despite the number of new companies making sneakers, Nike's brand means customers continue buying Nike's shoes over its cheaper competitors.

For a strong brand to equal a moat it must convey something that will stop a customer using a competitor. For example, Rolex and Tiffany convey status and prestige. A customer may be able to buy a cheaper watch or piece of jewellery but they choose these brands because of the power of the brand.

The important question to ask is: does this company's brand mean its customers will stay with it, even if prices rise significantly? If you answer yes to that question, then it is likely you've found a company with a strong moat.

4 Switching costs

Switching costs make it incredibly hard for a customer to leave once they are your customer.

The best example of switching costs is with telecommunication companies. Ever grown dissatisfied with your phone plan and tried to switch? Well, the first thing you have to do is pay out your plan. That cost of switching stops a lot of consumers moving to a different company, even if they're unhappy with their current provider.

Switching costs don't always have to be about money. They can be time- or effort-based as well. An example of this would be accounting software provider Xero. Businesses that are used to using Xero's accounting platform would be reluctant to change to another accounting platform because of the time it would take to transfer data over and get used to the new operating system.

Okay, you've found a moat: now what?

A moat is a great feature for a potential investment, but it isn't the be-all and end-all. If the company isn't using that moat to generate profit and then reinvesting that profit to grow, then the moat doesn't help much.

There are plenty of examples of companies that have let a moat go to waste. Two recent examples would be TripAdvisor and Yelp. TripAdvisor has an excellent network effect—as more users rate different attractions, restaurants and hotels, this adds value for every other user—yet its performance as a company has been less than stellar despite the strong network it has built up.

That's why moats are only part of the search for a great investment. But when you find a company with one, you can buy and hold it for years as it grows and grows, protected from competitors by its moat.

WARREN BUFFETT
find moats that can last

Warren Buffett is the world's most famous investor and the chairman and CEO of Berkshire Hathaway.

'The dynamics of capitalism guarantee that competitors will repeatedly assault any business "castle" that is earning high returns. Therefore a formidable barrier such as a company's being the low cost producer (GEICO, Costco) or possessing a powerful world-wide brand (Coca-Cola, Gillette, American Express) is essential for sustained success. Business history is filled with "Roman Candles", companies whose moats proved illusory and were soon crossed.'

Buffett's vice-president, **Charlie Munger**, has this to say:

'Frequently, you'll look at a business having fabulous results. And the question is, "How long can this continue?" Well, there's only one way I know to answer that. And that's to think about why the results are occurring now—and then to figure out the forces that could cause those results to stop occurring.'

Reduce the noise

We spoke about noise in Part 6, in the section on finding good investing information. As a recap, noise is unwanted, unnecessary information that only disrupts and clouds your longer-term thinking. Separating information flow so you can really focus on what matters will help you stick to your investing strategy, and control your emotions.

A lot of financial news headlines these days are emotionally charged to make you feel like you need to do something. 'ASX set to plunge at open', 'Billions wiped from markets', 'Retail suffering historic losses'—while these headlines might be right, you need to ask yourself: do they make a difference to your investment goal long term?

The ultimate goal of the media is not to help you with developing a long-term picture. It's to sell news. Imagine if the headline was 'Billions wiped from markets today, but don't worry, this is naturally part of the market cycle. Nothing to see here.'

It's not very sensationalist, but it would certainly help you keep a lot calmer, and put things in perspective.

At the end of the day, remember what investing is about. Looking for great long-term businesses that will earn profit year after year, and use that profit to grow their business. Whenever you see a news article about a company, always ask yourself, 'has this news fundamentally changed the business?'

Tips to reduce the 'noise'

There's no doubt that when we started, reducing the noise was very hard. It takes time. Once you become more confident in your strategy, and the path you want to take, it will become easier to filter information.

Lessons we've learnt to help block the noise:

- Don't look at your portfolio every day. Not worth it. Trust us.
- Keep your time horizon in focus—short-term volatility is natural in markets.
- Don't look at the headlines if the market is crashing; you may feel compelled to sell—this is the worst thing you can do!
- Question your thesis—have the reasons you initially invested changed? If not, it's noise—move on.
- Set aside time in your week to actually think and reflect on your investing journey.
- How much of your daily reading is short-term focused versus long-term? Get the balance right, so it's more meaningful.
- Trust data over narrative and anecdotes.
- Never listen to pundits, or your friends.
- Read broadly, and read information that doesn't match your thesis—challenge your beliefs and understand both sides.
- Be patient! Success is not gained in a day. Investing is a long-term game.

We love the chart below. It just highlights the importance of having a long-term focus. Having a mindset of investing for the future will help you to block out the day-to-day headlines.

Australian shares have climbed a wall of worry
All Ords price index

You can imagine the headlines that would have been flying around during all the major market crashes illustrated on this chart. You'd be forgiven if you thought the world was ending. But despite all the worry, and short-term pain, the Australian stock market has continued to recover, and reach new highs over the last 100 years.

Keep the big picture in focus.

 FROM THE EQUITY MATES
community

We asked the community about their approach to reducing noise:

'My view has matured though I'm sure I still don't know very much. I have the general ideas and concepts and apply those core parts to my strategy then try to block out noise, emotion and FOMO.'
DYLAN

'As I read more, I know I cannot hear all the noise. Start to choose the right people to follow.'
JENNIFER

'Try to block out the noise and stick to your own path.'
MEL

Boost returns

Given our time horizon, something we have come to understand is the power of leverage. Using leverage in your portfolio is a great way to boost your returns; but buyer beware.

What is leverage?

Leverage is borrowing money to increase the amount you invest in the market, above what you could invest with just your own money. The idea is that by getting a larger exposure, you can make more money. But, like anything associated with investing, and especially borrowing money, it does come with increased risks.

How does it work?

We'll use an example to demonstrate leverage in one of its simplest forms.

You have $500 to invest in JB Hi-Fi shares at, for argument's sake, $10 a share. You'd get 50 shares.

If the shares go up $2, you'll make $100 profit ($2 × 50 shares). If the shares go down $2, you'll lose $100.

If you wanted to leverage to try to boost your portfolio, you could borrow money to increase the size of that position. Say you borrowed $500 (of, course highly unlikely the bank would lend you such a small amount, but stay with us here—it's just an example!).

Now you have a total of $1,000 to invest in JB Hi-Fi, getting you 100 shares.

If the shares go up $2, you'll now make $200 in profit. But, as you can see, if they go down $2, you'll lose $200 (twice as much as before) *and* you will still owe the bank the $500 that you borrowed.

So it goes both ways. You need to understand what you are doing, and the risks, before you even consider leverage.

Thinking about leverage

People wouldn't think twice about borrowing up to their eyeballs to buy a house, yet they don't think about borrowing to invest in stocks in the same way. With a very long-term horizon, leverage can be a very powerful element in your portfolio once you understand how to manage it.

The advantages of leverage

- You have greater exposure to the market, so your returns can be increased.
- Interest rates are low in Australia, and look like they will be for a while—money is cheap.
- Getting large exposure early in your investing journey can help maximise the impact of compounding over a long time horizon.
- It's cheaper to borrow to invest in stocks than it is to invest in a house.

The disadvantages of leverage

- Your losses can become big, very quickly.
- You can lose a lot of money.
- You need to know what you're doing—you can lose money.
- Oh, and if you're unsure about leverage, stay away—you can lose money.

Do I need leverage?

The short answer: no. You can live a long and happy investing life and make a lot of money without using leverage.

Leverage can be a useful tool, but don't feel like you need it for your investing returns. If you are interested, we outline a few of the ways you can use it below.

What are your options to leverage?

Product	Description	Can you lose more than you invested? (i.e. owe money)
Margin loan	Borrow money to invest. You pay interest on your loan until you pay it back.	Yes
Principal and interest loan	Borrow money to invest. You pay the loan back over time at a set rate (similar to a mortgage)	Yes
Leveraged ETF	Buy an ETF on the stock market and the ETF provider then borrows money to add to the investment.	No

Leverage isn't something we considered at all at the start of our investing journey. It was only after talking to hundreds of experienced investors and fund managers, doing hours of research and understanding how it fitted with our investing strategy that we have started to appreciate the benefits (and also the risks).

WARREN BUFFETT
on leverage

In his 2010 shareholder letter, Warren Buffett made these remarks about the dangers of leverage.

'When leverage works, it magnifies your gains. Your spouse thinks you're clever, and your neighbours get envious. But leverage is addictive. Once having profited from its wonders, very few people retreat to more conservative practices. And as we all learned in third grade—and some relearned in 2008—any series of positive numbers, however impressive the numbers may be, evaporates when multiplied by a single zero. History tells us that leverage all too often produces zeroes, even when it is employed by very smart people.'

Forget stock picking

Not a lot of new content will be introduced here but we just want to reiterate the point—don't stress about picking the perfect stock—just get started!

Too often people agonise over what to buy. Or feel like they don't know enough to start. There are enough options available today that there is no excuse not to start. In fact, you can build a very successful, diversified portfolio without ever having to pick one single stock.

We both fell foul of trying to pick stocks when we started. We were going for the hero shot, hoping to make a fortune. As you would expect, a lot of the shots didn't pay off. Now, we're not saying avoid stock picking altogether. For some of you, it may be all you do; you may be great at it or you just love the chase.

But for many of you, it's a barrier. Don't get caught up trying to pick the perfect stock. *Just get started!*

Here are three of the key lessons we've learnt, and wish we had known before we started—the details of which we have covered earlier:

1 Look for ETFs, LICs, fund managers and investing apps that can do the picking for you.
2 Just get some sort of exposure. There are enough opportunities for you to access the market without needing to stress about picking stocks.
3 You won't always get it right.

Here's a fun fact for you to ponder . . .

Warren Buffett has always been critical of the fees that hedge funds and fund managers charge. In 2008 he issued a challenge to the industry—that an S&P 500 index fund would outperform a handpicked portfolio of stocks, including fees, costs and expense, over a ten-year period.

The bet? One million dollars.

Ted Seides, co-founder of Protégé Partners, took on the bet.

Not too soon after they made the bet, the Global Financial Crisis hit, and the market tanked. This is where the hedge fund excelled, and the index bombed: −37%, compared to the hedge fund's −23.9%.

But from that point on, the S&P 500 index fund outperformed the handpicked portfolio of the hedge fund.

Seides conceded before the ten years was up, admitting he'd lost. The index fund had gained $854,000, compared to Protégé's $220,000.

Moral of the story? Not even the pros can beat the market, so don't stress about trying to do it yourself. Market returns are more than satisfactory.

FROM THE EXPERTS
beating the market

Meir Statman is an economist and the Glenn Klimek Professor of Finance at Santa Clara University. This what he has to say on picking stocks to try to beat the market.

'The answer, unfortunately, is not in one sentence. But, if I had to say one sentence it's that for individual investors it is useful to think about the market as being efficient. Period.

What it means for me and for you is don't try to beat the market. Stay away from any advice that says pick these stocks or those, pick this active mutual fund or that, because you are going to be at the losing end.

Then when I say losing end, I'm not suggesting that people will actually lose money, but rather they will come behind people who just put their money in an index fund and just buy and hold and eventually use the money for retirement or to buy a house or whatever it is for.

And so the answer for people like us, meaning individuals, amateurs, is to stay away from trends to try to beat the market. That is, you have to understand the ecology of the markets. There are predators and there are prey.

The predators are professionals. They have unique information that is not available to you. It is not something that you will read in the newspaper or hear on television. They have a deep understanding of the industry they are covering and so on. And they trade with people who are in fact the prey.

And remember, in every trade there is an idiot. And if you don't know who it is, you ask yourself whenever you are about to trade, who is the idiot on the other side of the trade?

Or using another analogy—realise that trading is like playing tennis, not against the wall, but against an opponent on the other side, whom you've never met before and you don't recognise and you don't know their skills. And so it might well be [the tennis star] Djokovic on the other side. [Your chance of] Winning is not fifty–fifty. I get into a game when it is not just for fun. Let's say that it is $100,000 that goes from the loser to the winner. Well, it's very clear that you are going to be losing that money. And unless it is worth it to you, $100,000 to play with Djokovic, or to lose to Djokovic, don't do it.'

Section summary
YOUR PROGRESS

☑ WHY INVEST
☑ BUILD AN INVESTOR MINDSET
☑ GET YOUR MONEY RIGHT
☑ UNDERSTANDING THE BASICS
☑ TAKING THE PLUNGE
☑ BEYOND THE FIRST INVESTMENT

☑ LESSONS WE WISH WE HAD KNOWN

We've learnt a lot since we started investing. In this section we covered all the key lessons we wish we had known when we got started. Many of them we learnt the hard way (by losing money). By reading this section hopefully you learnt them the easy way and can avoid our mistakes.

You have:

✓ understood the importance of looking outside Australia for investing opportunities
✓ learnt how you can build good investing habits: keep it simple, reduce the noise and get out of your own way
✓ explored some of the key factors that make a great company: great management and a strong moat
✓ understood that you don't need to pick individual stocks to enjoy the benefits of investing.

☐ PULLING IT ALL TOGETHER

PART 9

Pulling It All Together

Bad news, you've made it to the end of *Get Started Investing*. Good news, your investing journey is just beginning.

What have you learnt?

There are plenty of reasons to not invest. We hope Get Started Investing *has given you one big one to invest.*

Getting started investing is within your grasp. The obstacles can be overcome. They are not mountains, not even molehills. Technology has bulldozed them all and made investing as easy as downloading an app.

As you go on your investing journey, you'll look back and regret not starting earlier. You'll think back to the reasons that held you back and wonder why they ever stopped you. Don't forget them. Use them as a reminder to pass on your knowledge (or this book) to a friend or a loved one. Too many Australians never get started and miss out on the awesome wealth-creating power of the stock market. Help make the next generation of Australians the most financially savvy who have ever existed.

We've covered a lot in *Get Started Investing* but these four lessons stand out as critical.

1 Investing is within your grasp

If there is one thing you remember once you put this book down, we hope it is this. Investing is for everyone. It has never been easier to get started and you have all the knowledge you need.

Even if you start small, with nothing more than a few cents, your future self will thank you. Regularly contributing small amounts to your investing accounts can grow into something meaningful in time.

2 Become a constant learner

Forget the idea that you need to know everything on day one. Investing is a lifelong journey. Everyone makes mistakes along the way, and everyone has a horror story about a big mistake they've made. That's okay. A mistake will not overturn a lifetime of good investing habits.

So get saving, get investing and get reading. We hope *Get Started Investing* has sparked an interest that will pay dividends (literally).

3 Understand what you're buying

The stock market can seem alien. Full of stock ticker codes, confusing charts and meaningless jargon. But, when you look beneath the surface, all you are doing is buying an ownership stake in a company. You are looking for companies that are run by great people, that are creating products and services that people want to buy and that have the opportunity to take their profits and grow their business.

4 Get rich slow

The power of compounding is something to behold. Over a lifetime it can turn small amounts of money into a comfortable retirement. It can turn your pay cheque into your nest egg.

Investing isn't a 'get rich quick' scheme. It requires consistency and patience. If you can focus on getting rich slowly, you just might do it.

Where to from here?

If you've enjoyed *Get Started Investing*, you'll love the Equity Mates community. Join over 200,000 like-minded Australians on their investing journey. Share thoughts, ask questions and continue building your investing knowledge.

From our five top-rated podcasts, a daily video show and plenty of other resources, Equity Mates has the resources to help you continue learning about investing.

To join the community, head to **www.equitymates.com**.

EquityMates

Just do it

We can't say it enough. Just get started.

At this point there is nothing left to say. You've got this!

Dip your toe in the water, and before you know it you'll be diving right in.

You'll make some mistakes, you'll learn some lessons the hard way, but you'll never look back. Taking control of your financial future is an empowering step to take. It's also a fun one!

There's nothing more to say.

Just get started!

Acknowledgements

Does anyone actually read the acknowledgements?

We should start by thanking you, those readers kind enough to read the (most) self-indulgent part of this book.

We are immensely grateful to so many people for helping us with this book and in our journey with Equity Mates. To our families—Jane, Peter, Kate and Georgie, and Ann, Tim and Claire—your support over the years has been incredible. To Bryce's partner, Harriet, our friends and to all those we've spoken to for a little too long about ETFs and LICs, thank you for your patience and your support.

This book would not have been possible without the support of the Equity Mates community. We started the podcast with no idea what it would become or the community that would get behind us. We cannot express how incredible the journey has been. You joined us when our audio quality was terrible, and the editing somehow made it worse. It means a lot that you have stuck with us. We hope you have all got something out of this book.

A huge thanks to all of the experts that have given up their time to share their insights with us. The world is a richer place when those with knowledge share it. Through the podcast you have helped all of the Equity Mates community build their knowledge and become better investors. For that, we say a massive thank you.

To the team at Allen & Unwin, especially Elizabeth, Angela and Richard, thank you for helping shape our ideas into this book. We hope you'll have us back for a second.

Finally, we want to acknowledge all of those financial advisors, writers, podcasters, YouTubers and everyone else who is working to improve the financial literacy of everyday Australians. It can often be a thankless task, but it is an important one. The benefits of investing can be generational, and together we hope we can work towards improving Australia's financial literacy. At some point, we hope it will be taught in schools. Until then, we see you. Keep up the great work.

Index